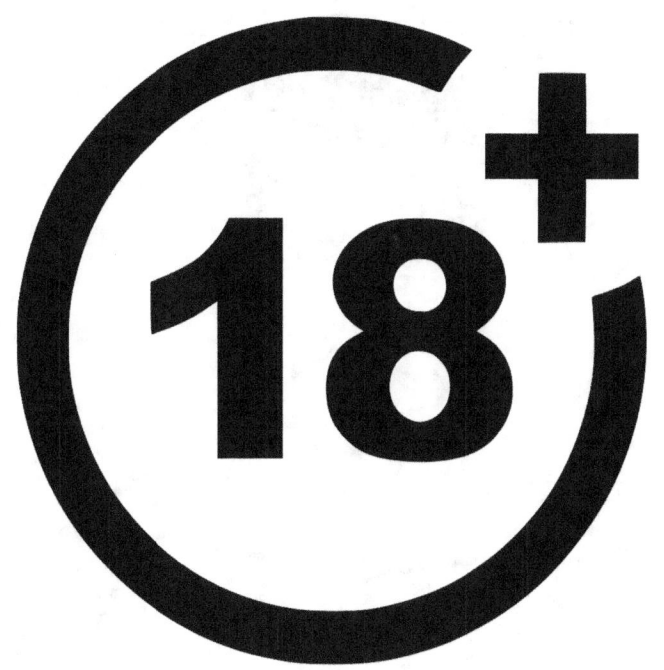

This coloring book is intended for adults aged 18 and above.

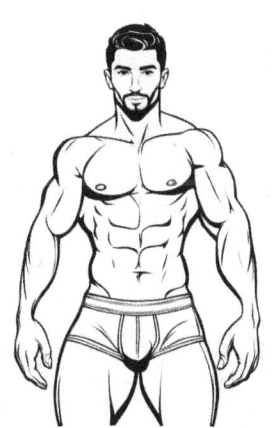

Copyright © 2023 Canvas Merchant. All rights reserved. No part of this coloring book may be reproduced in any form or by any means without prior written permission from the copyright owner. Unauthorized copying or distribution of this book is illegal, and violators will be prosecuted to the fullest extent of the law.

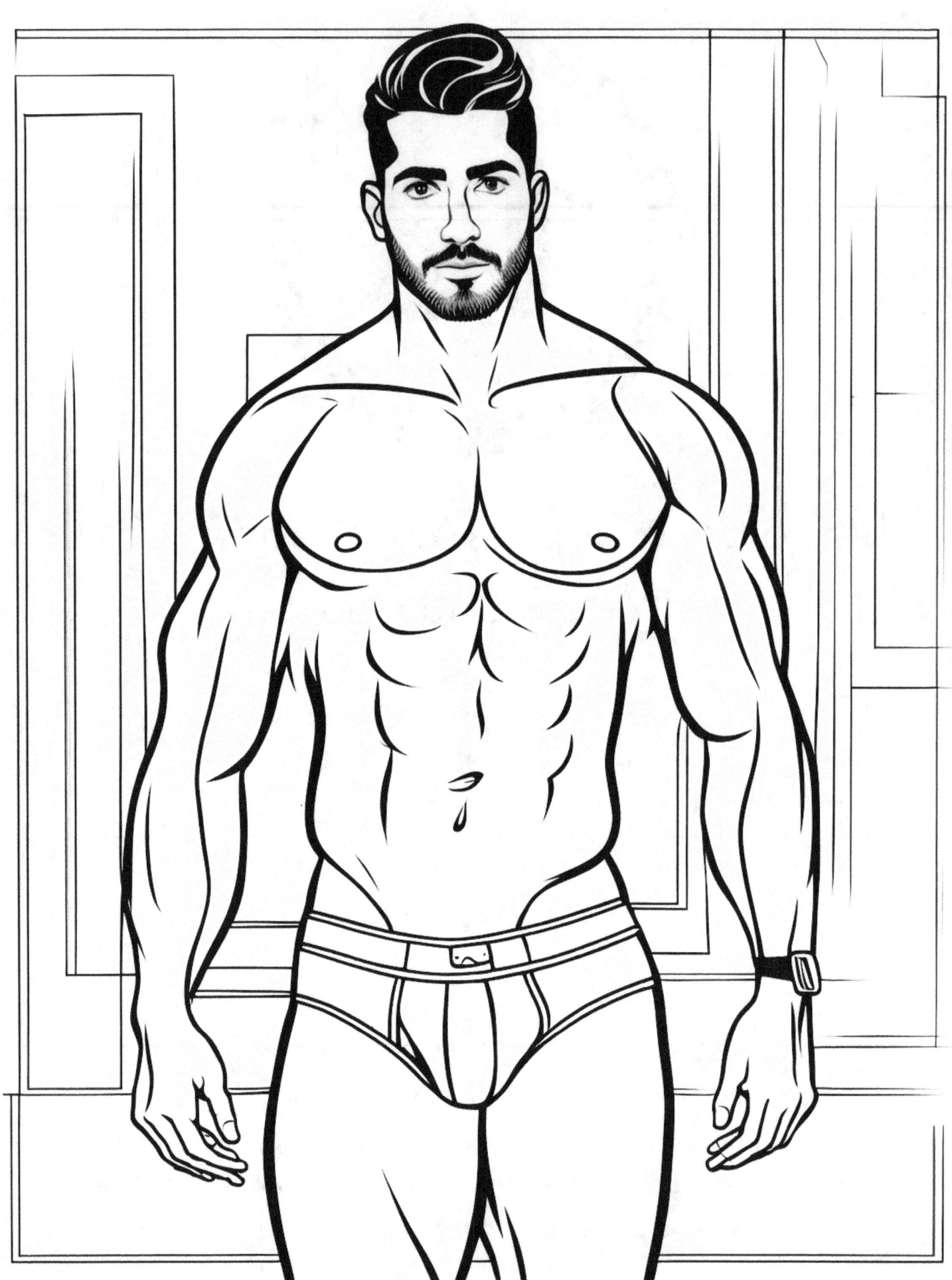

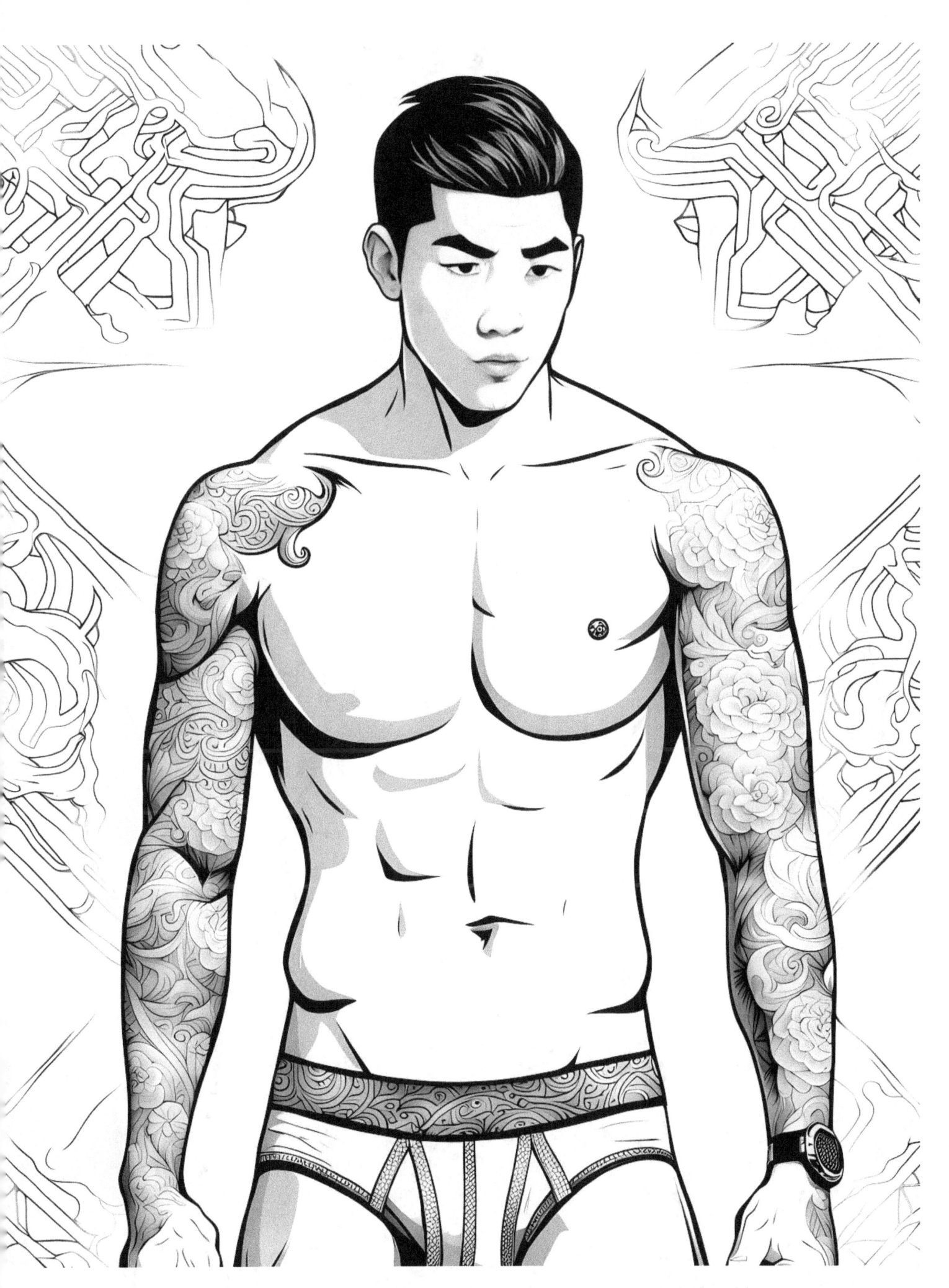

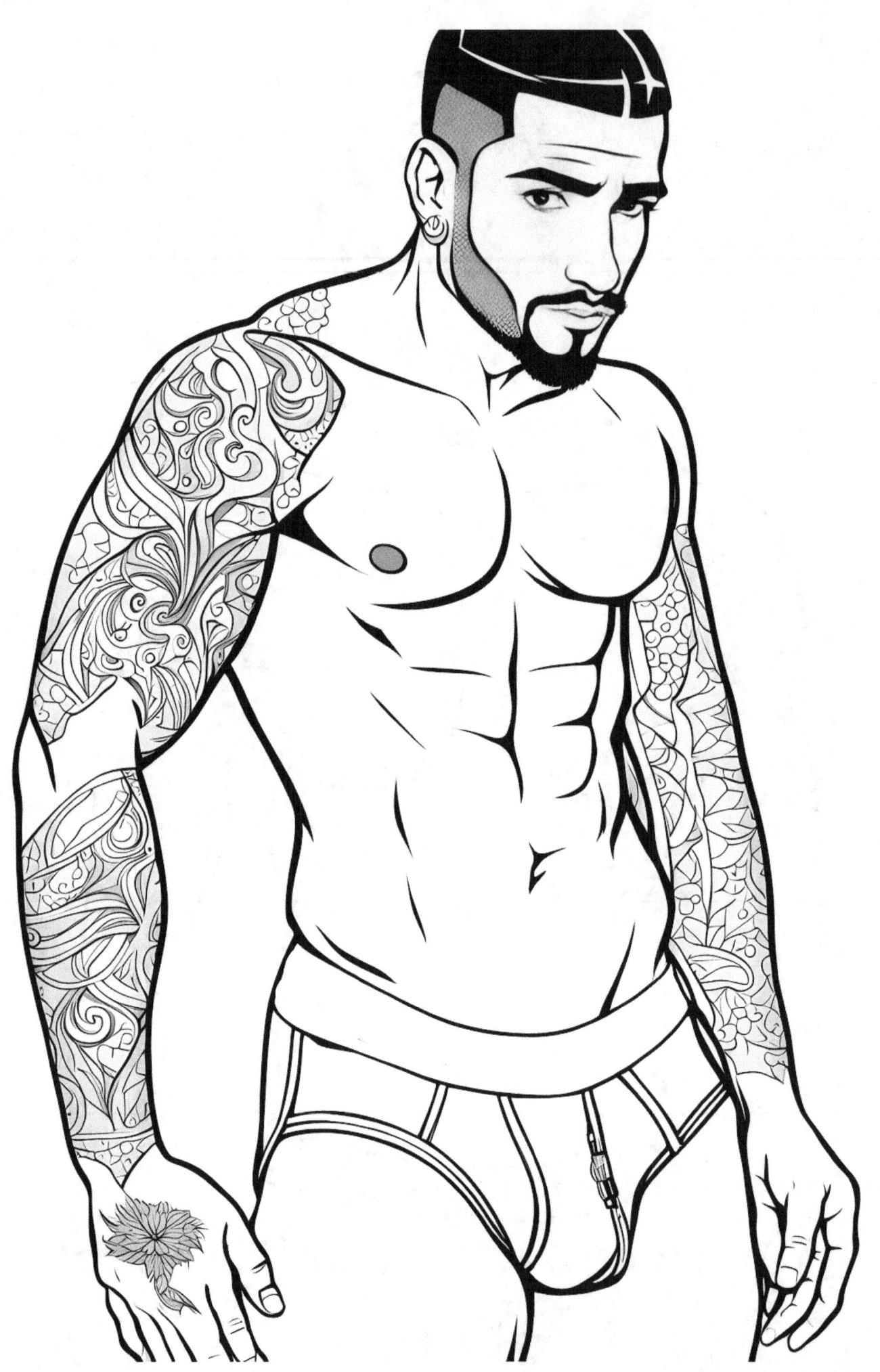

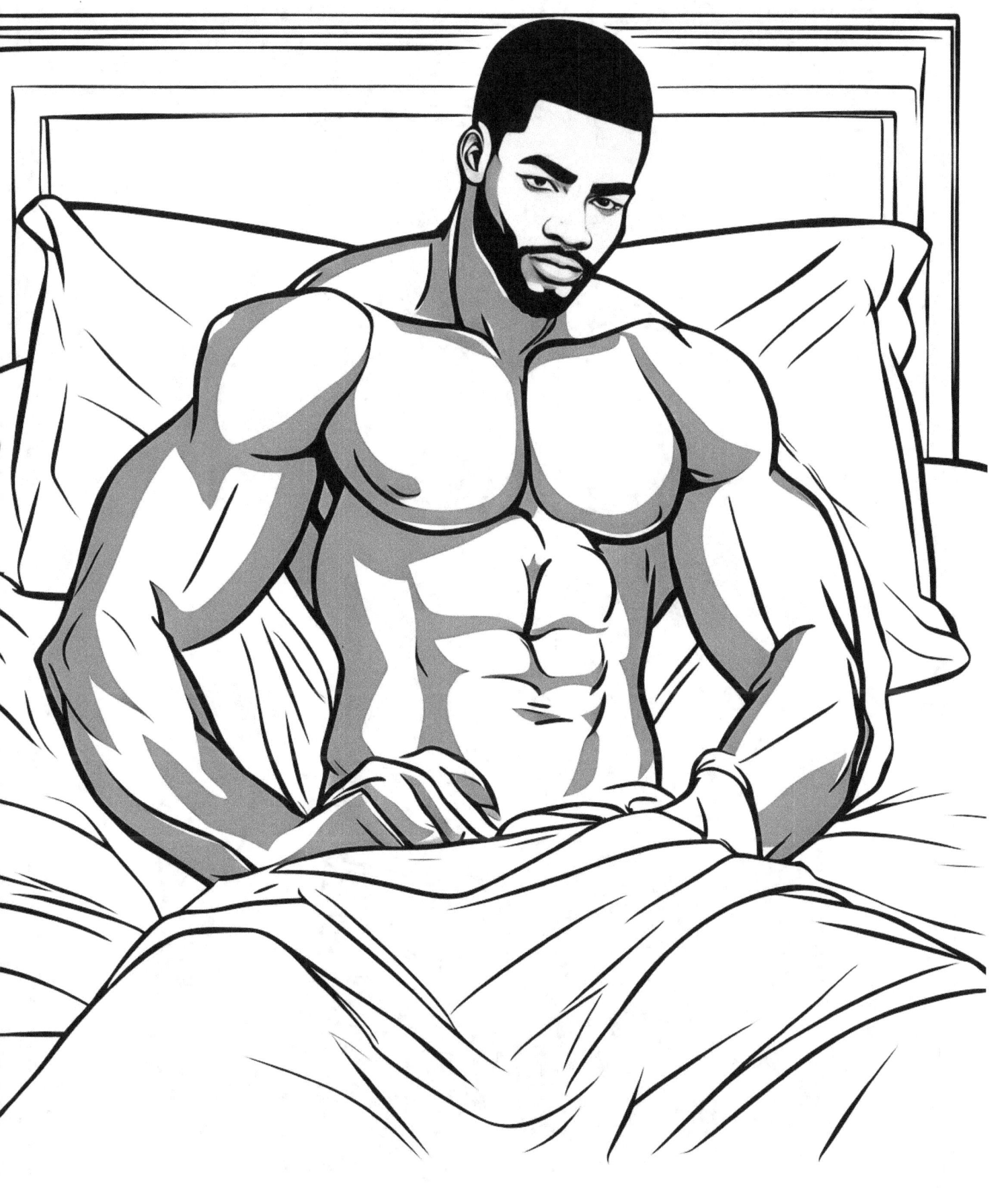

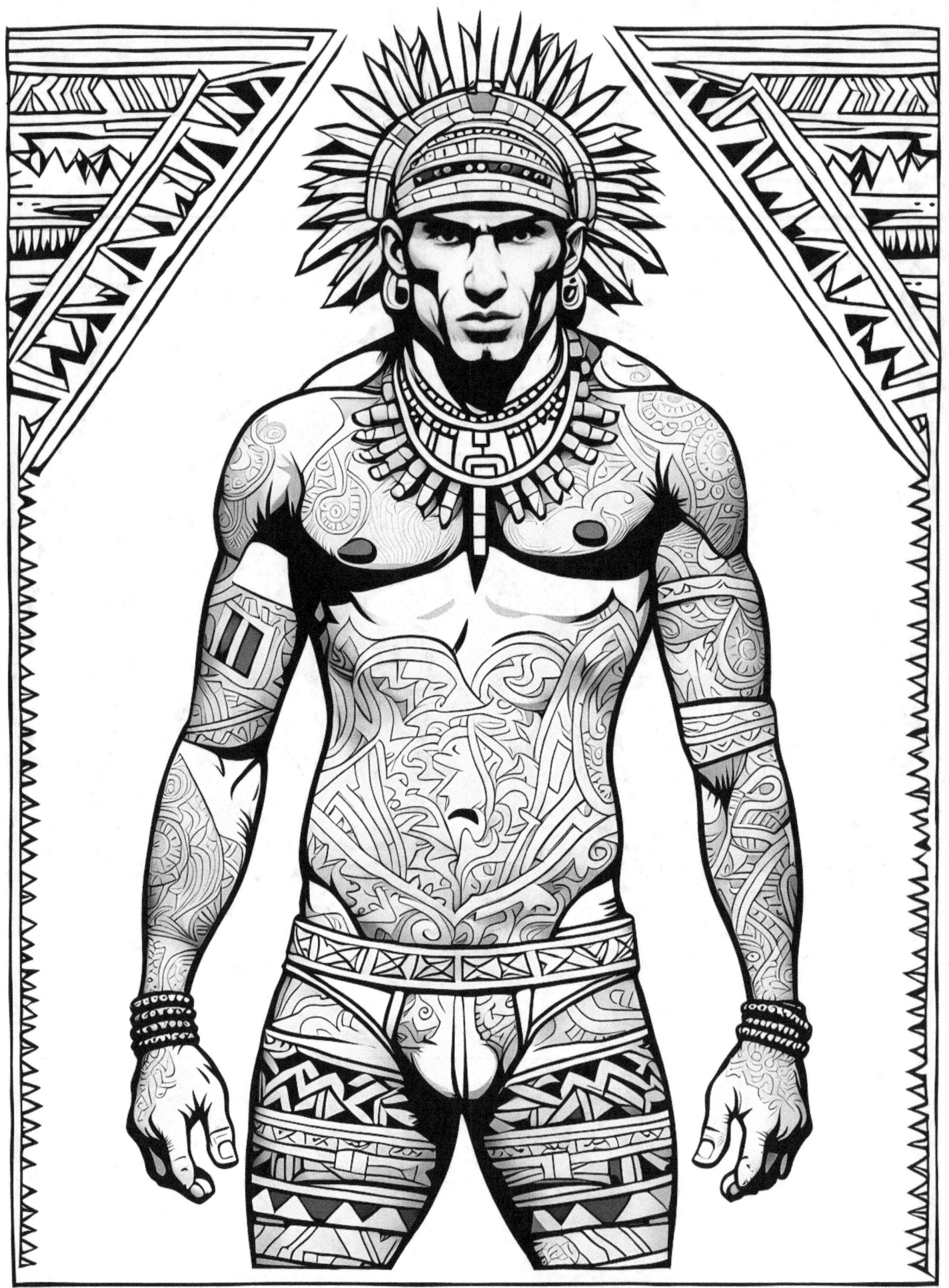

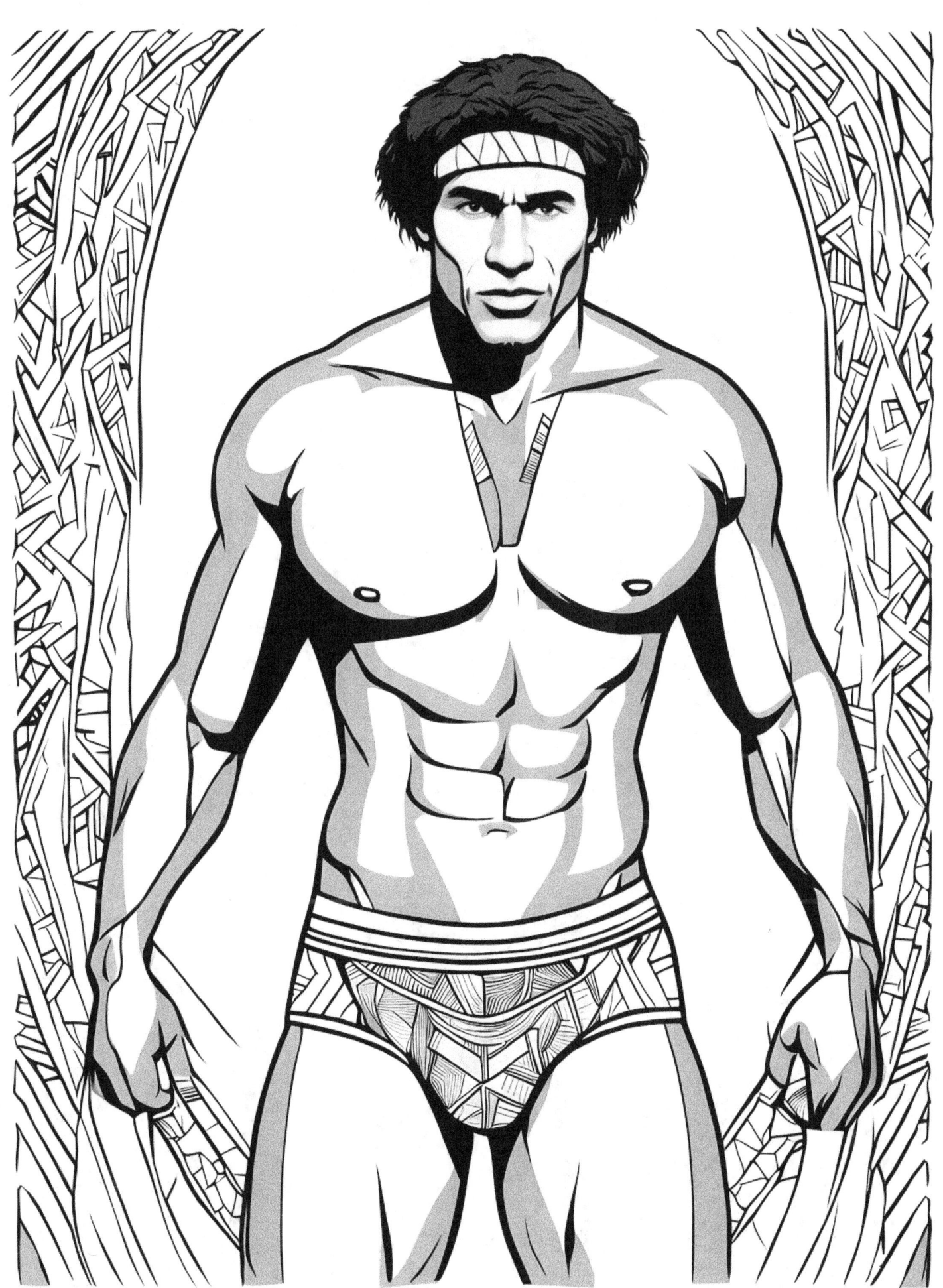

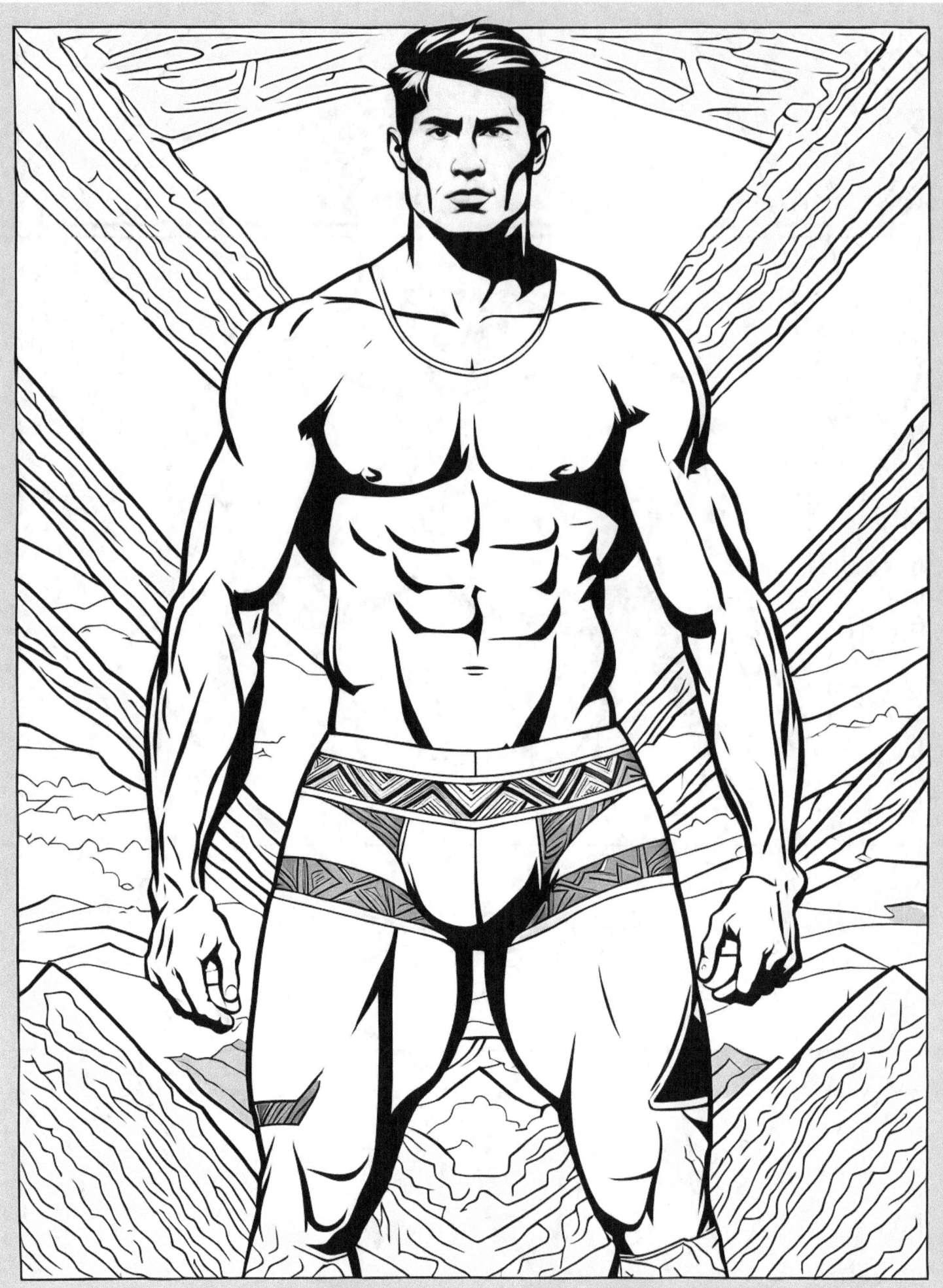

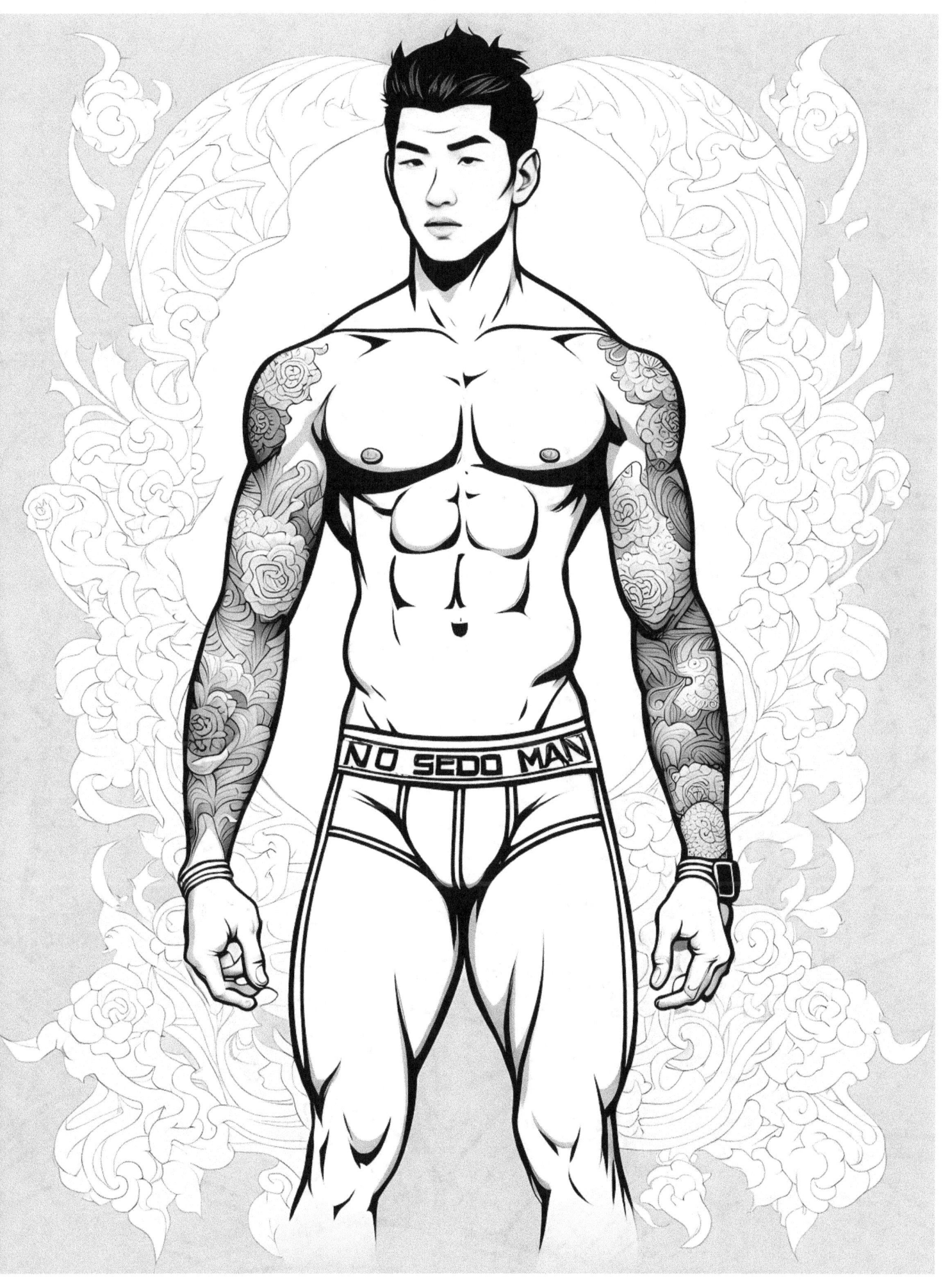

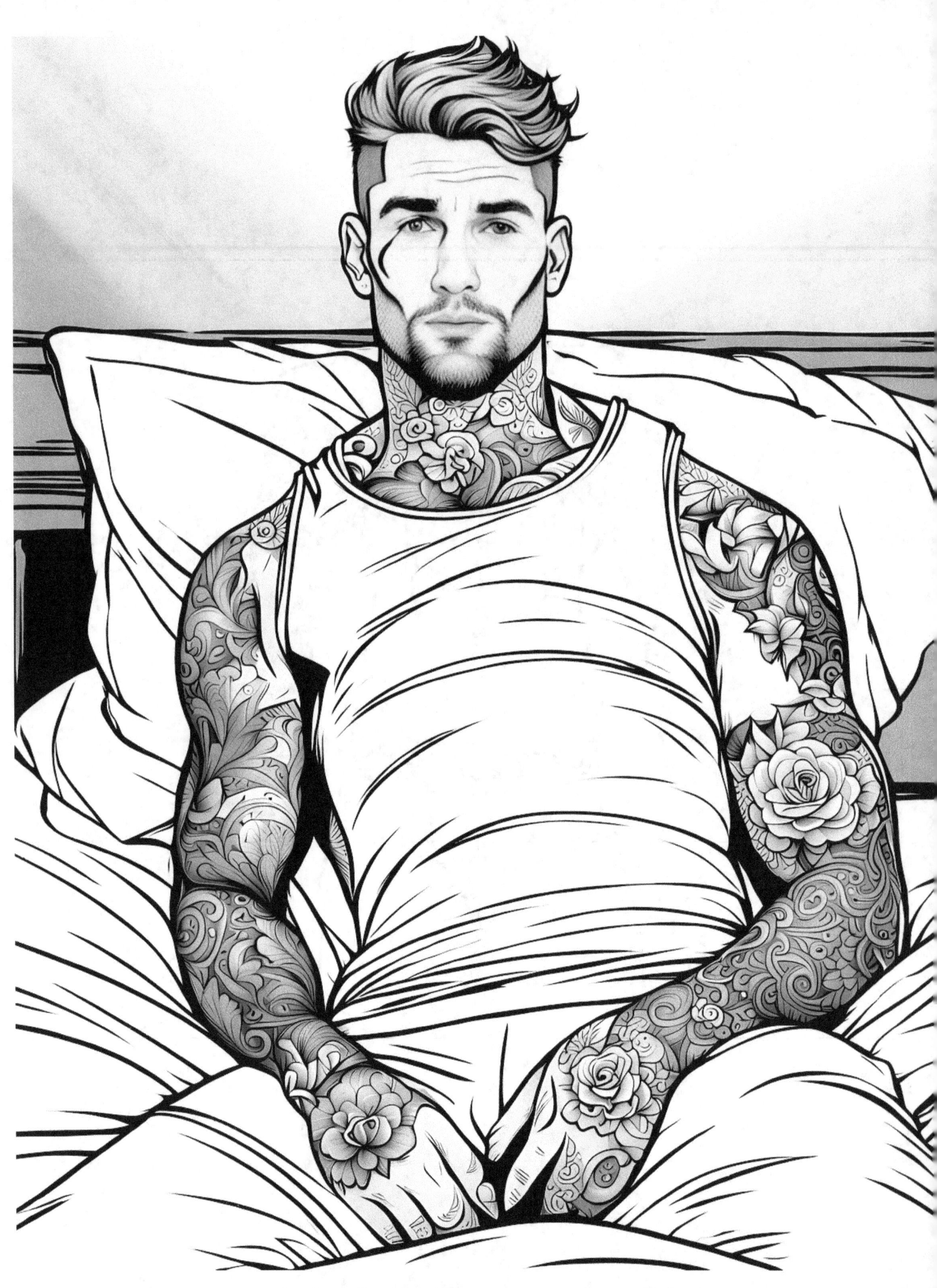

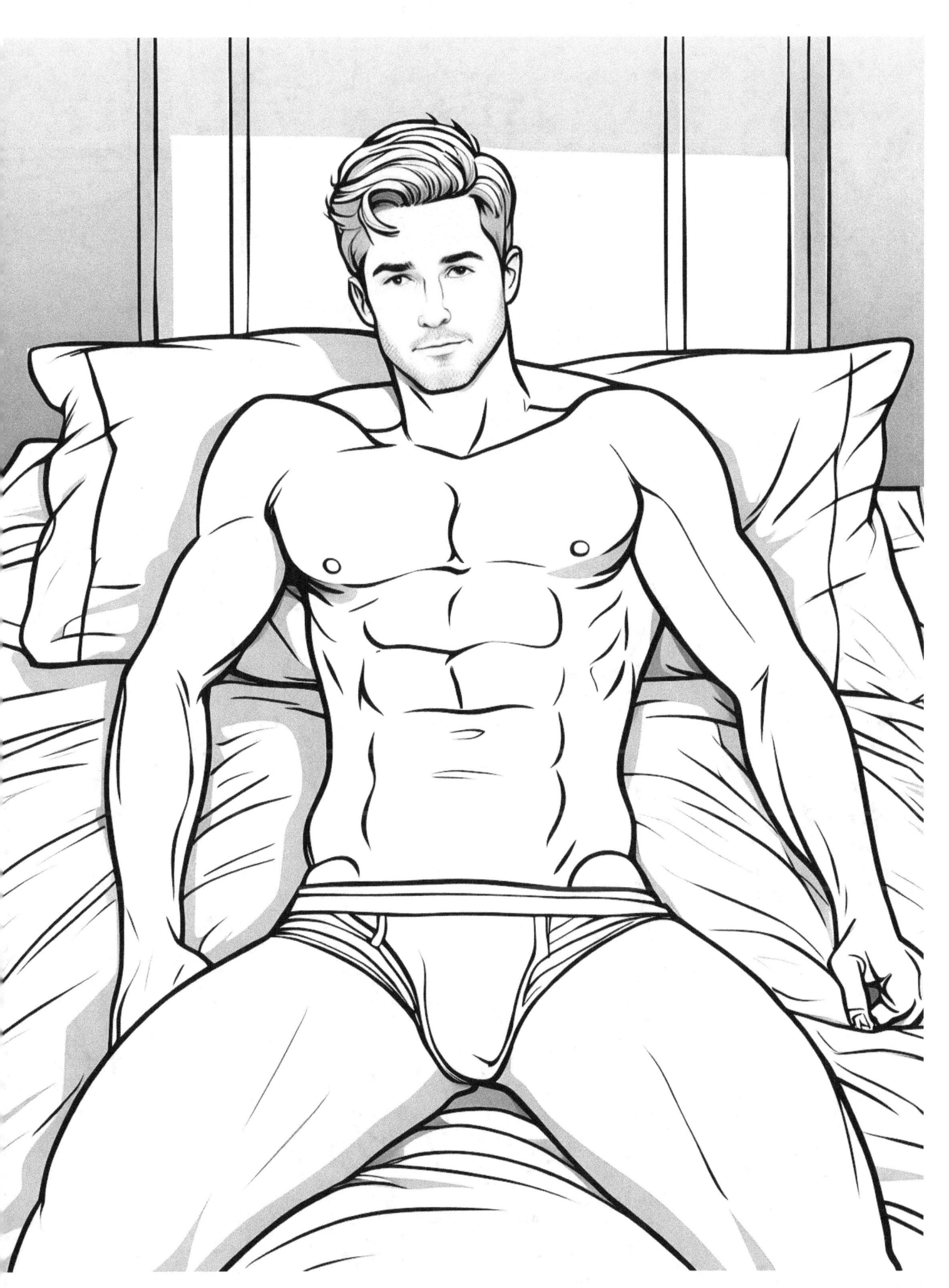

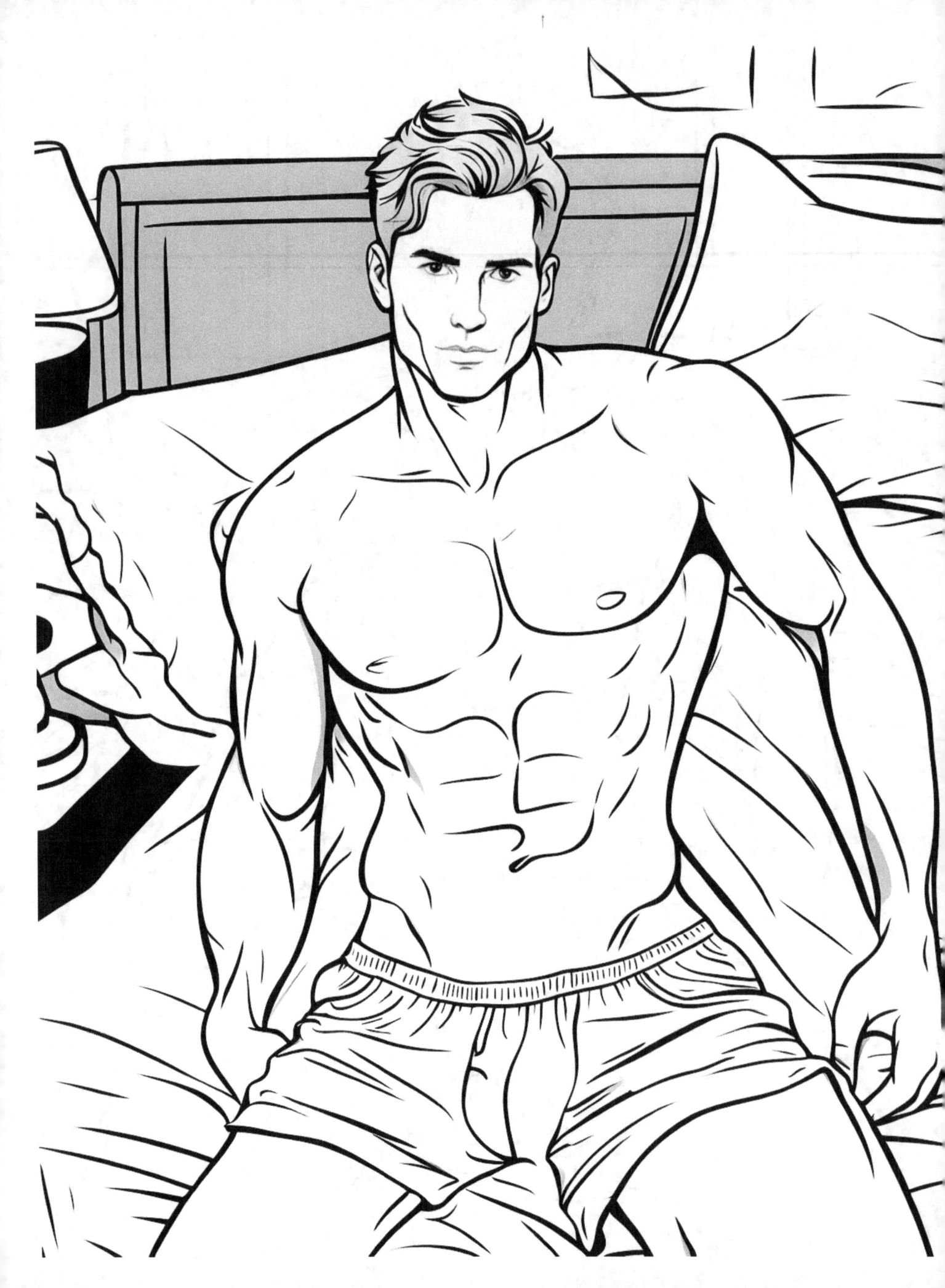

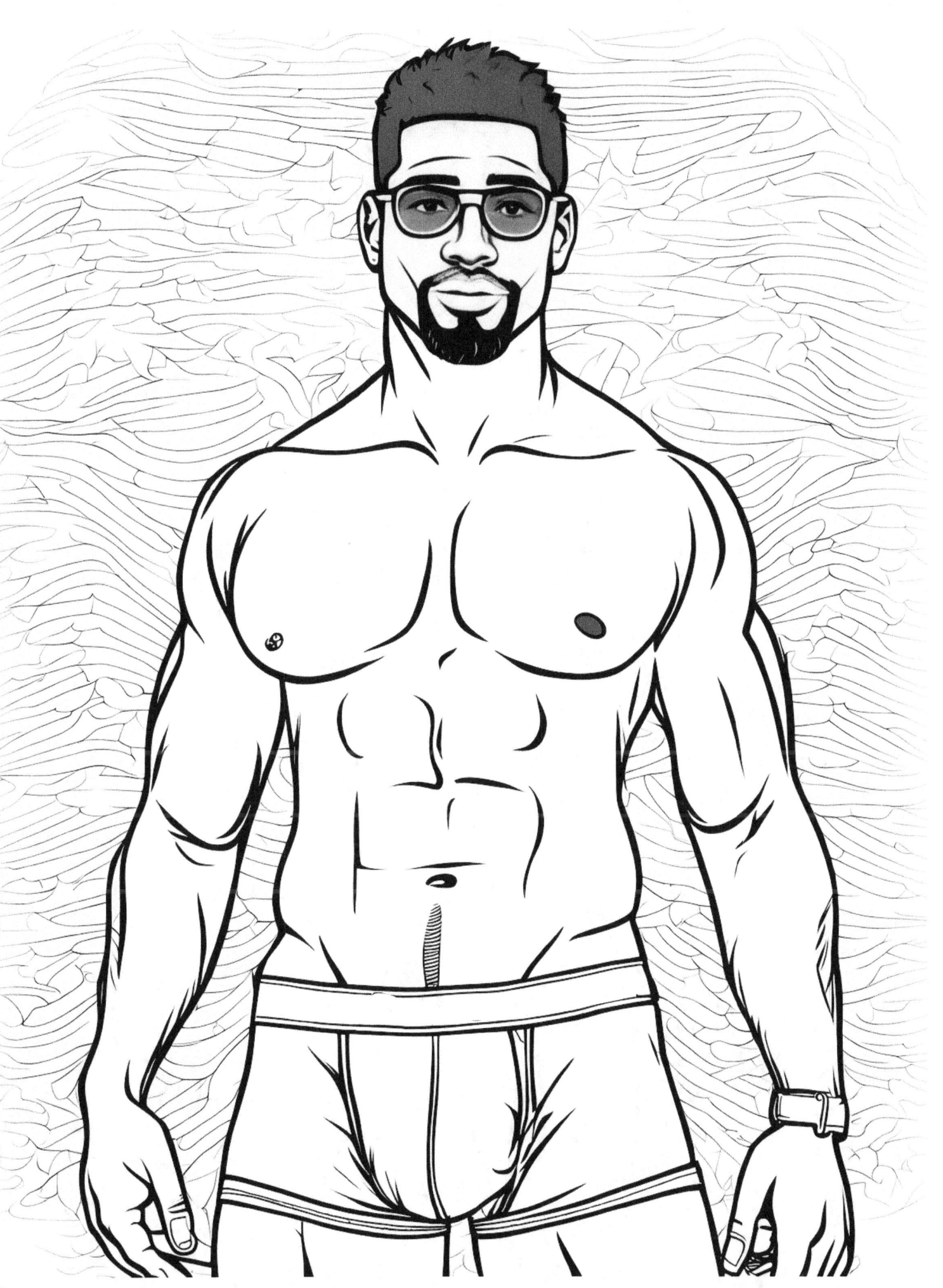

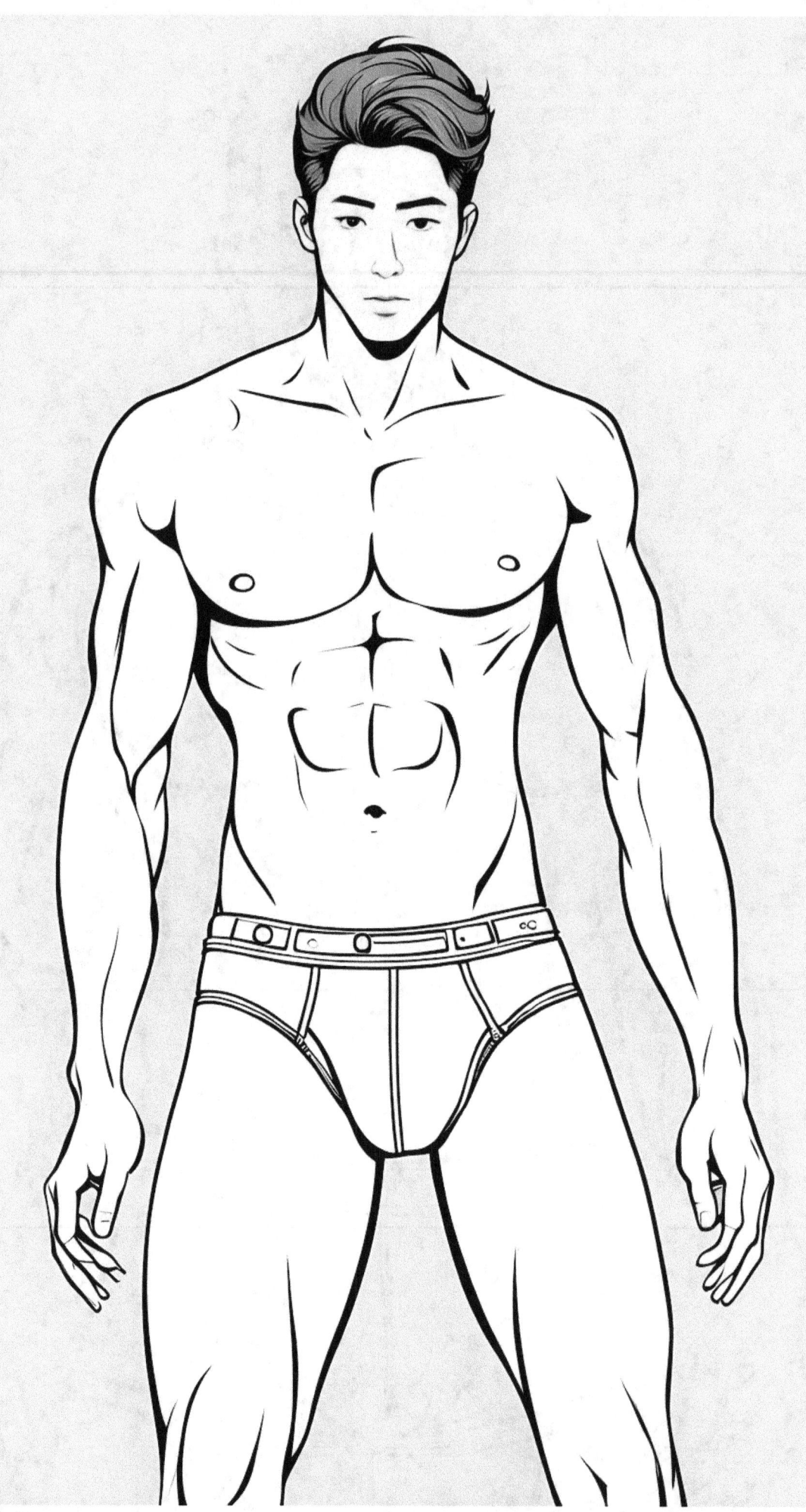

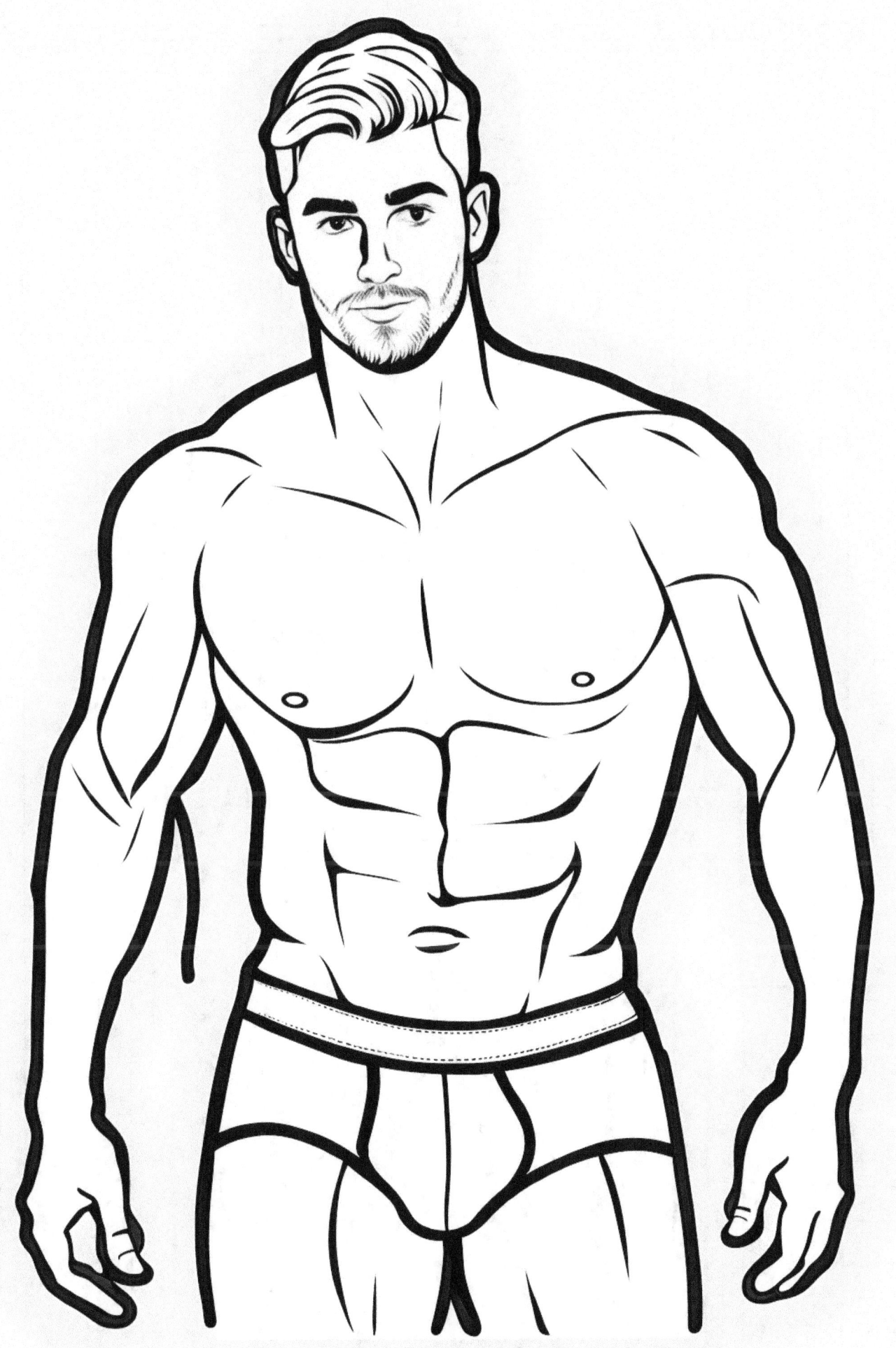

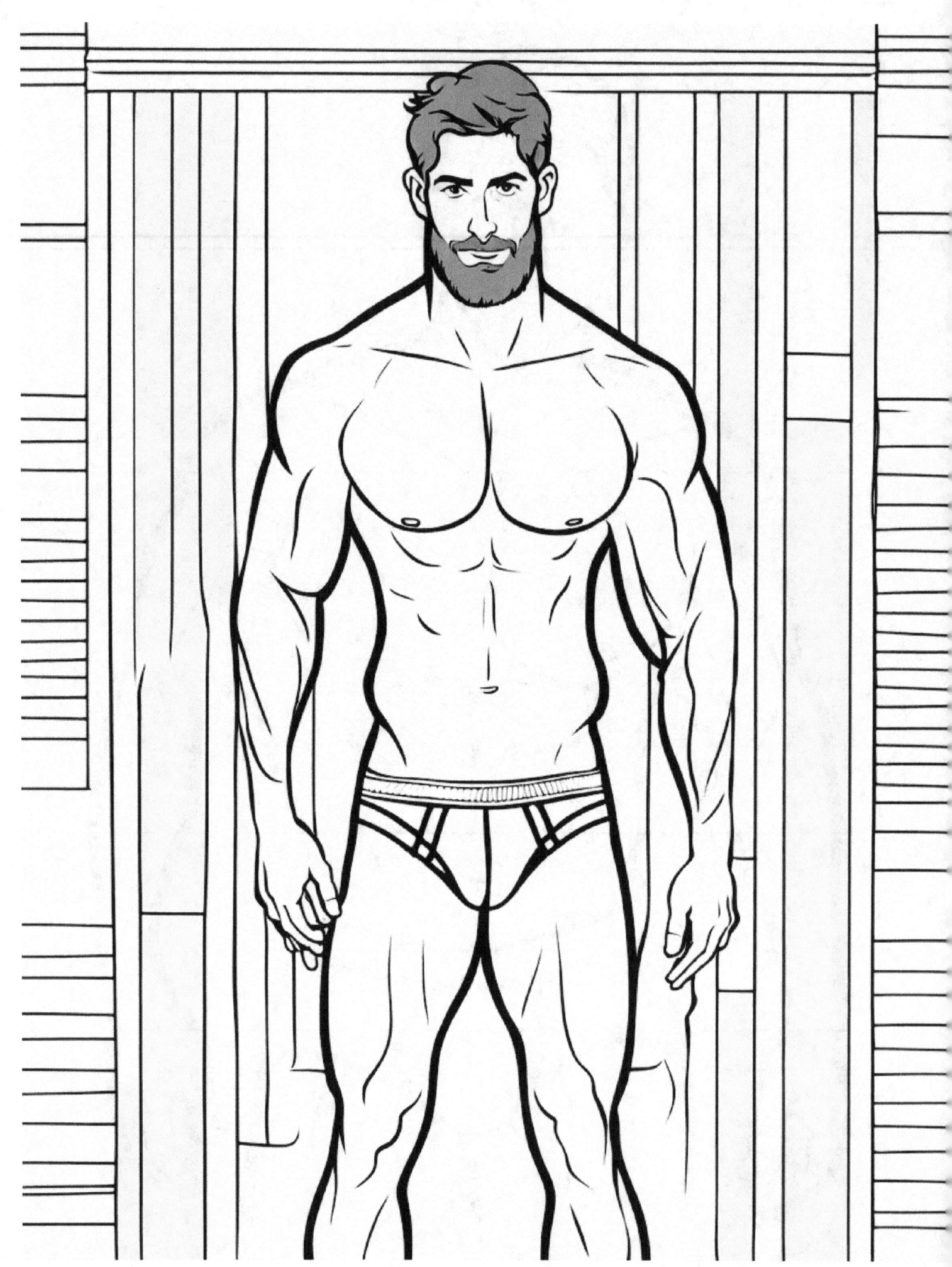

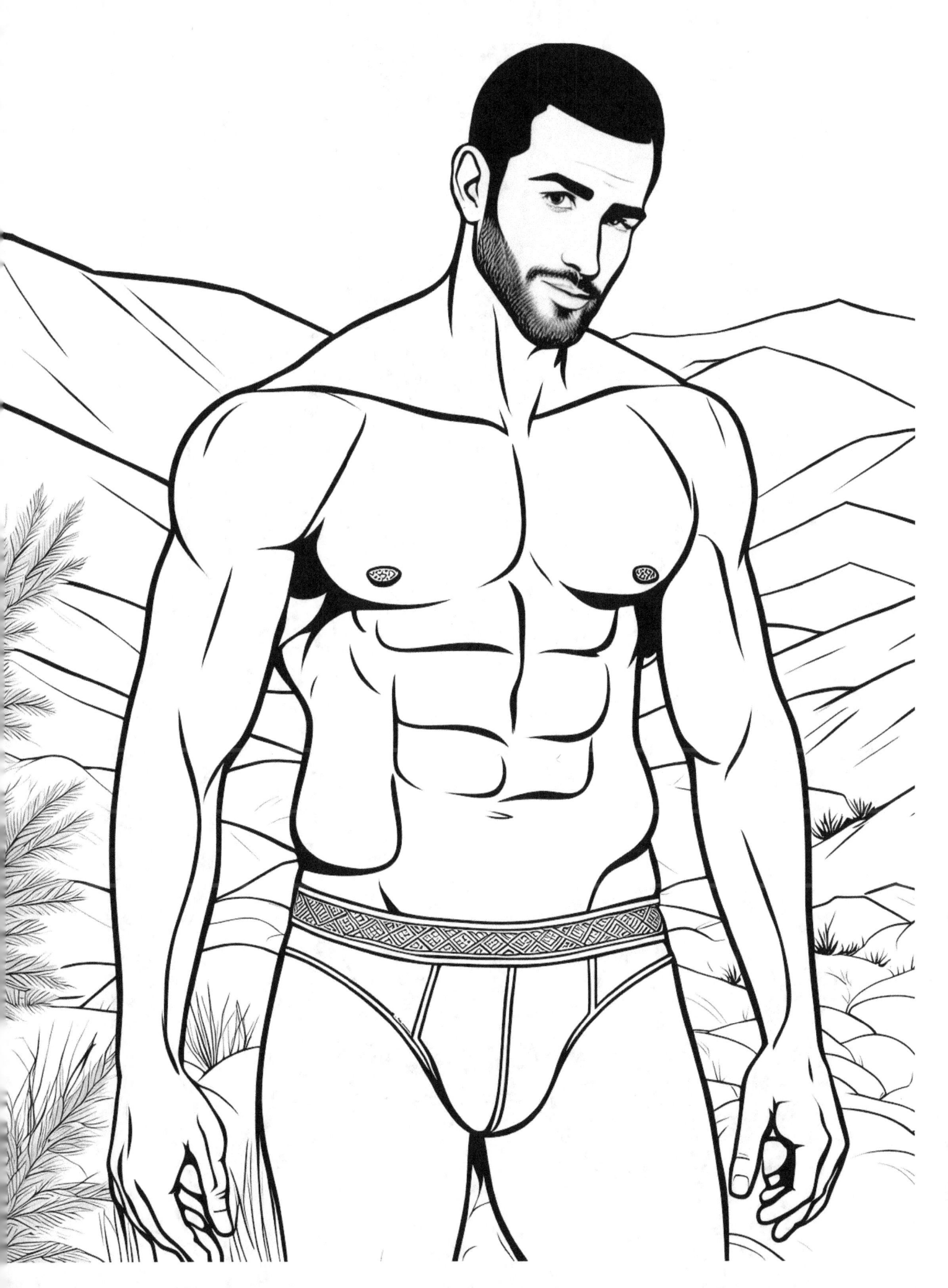

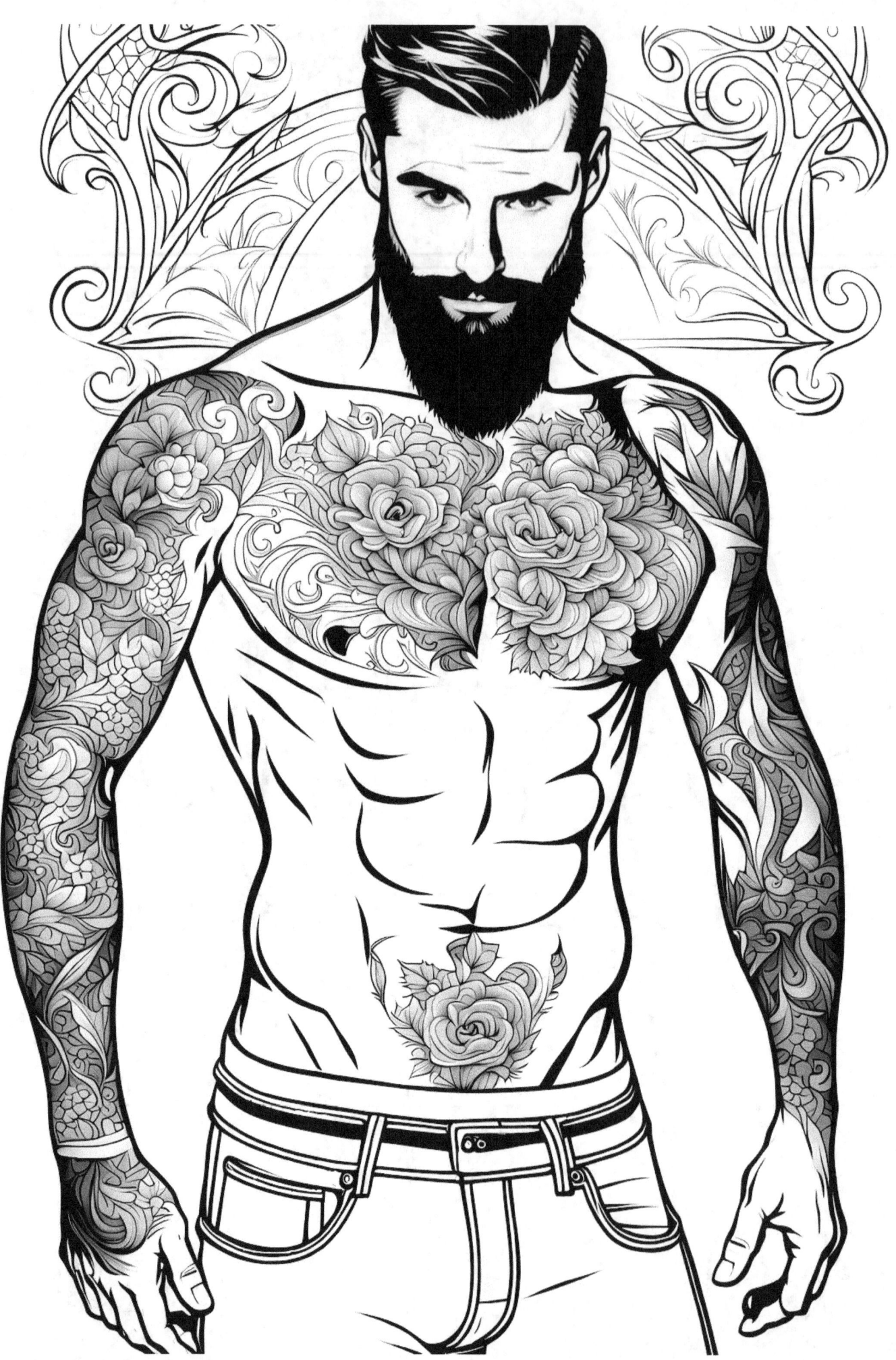

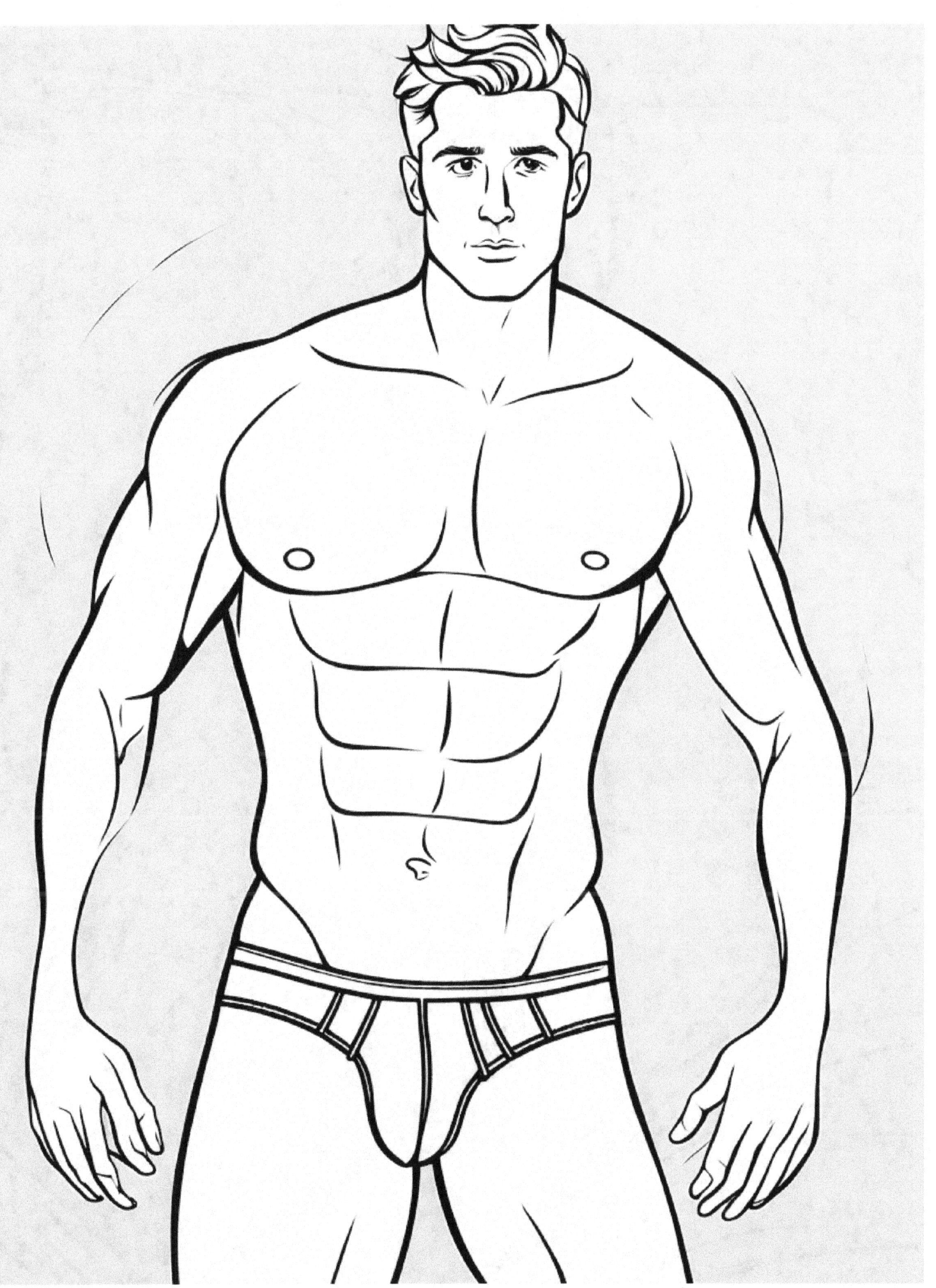

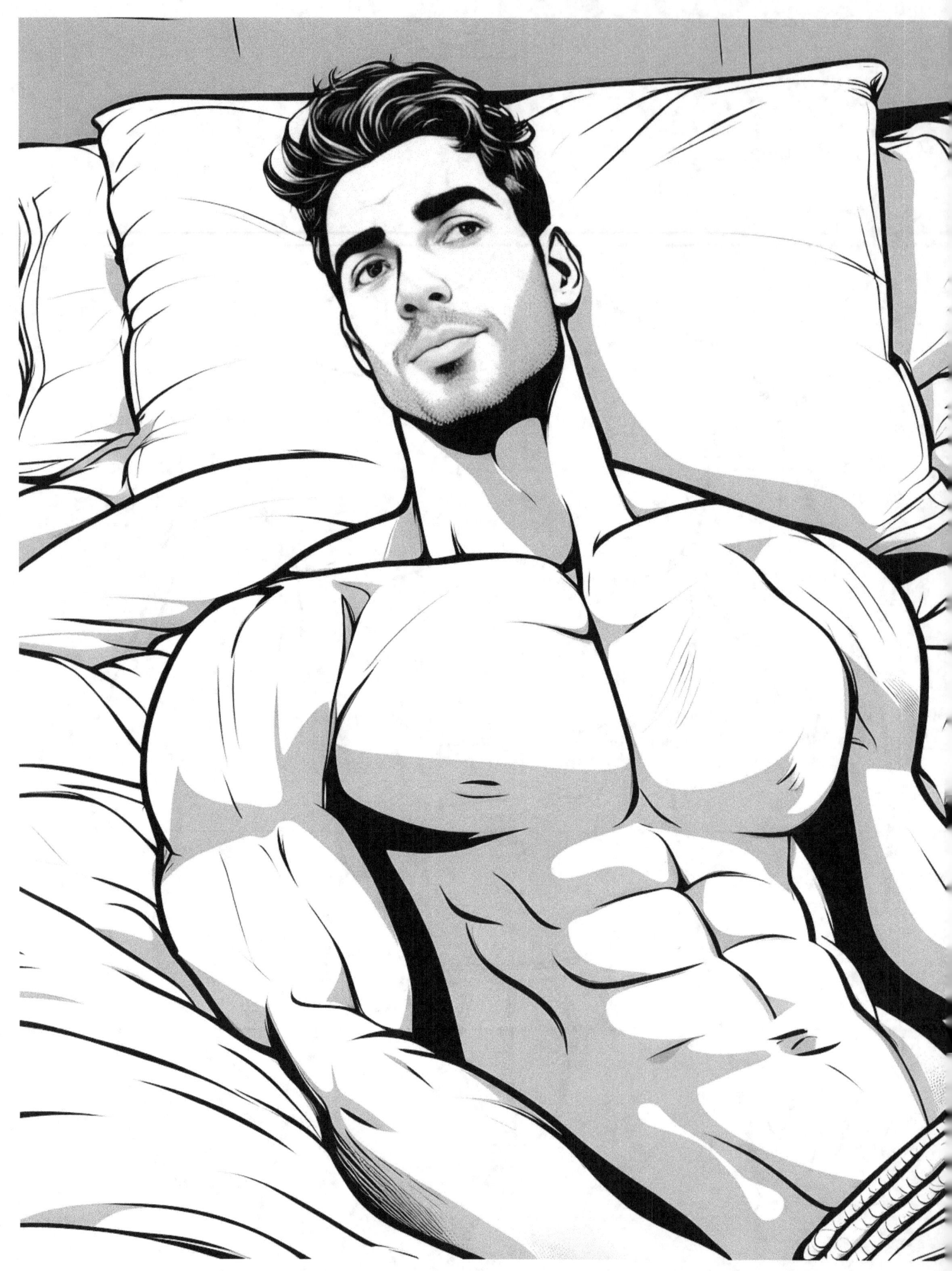

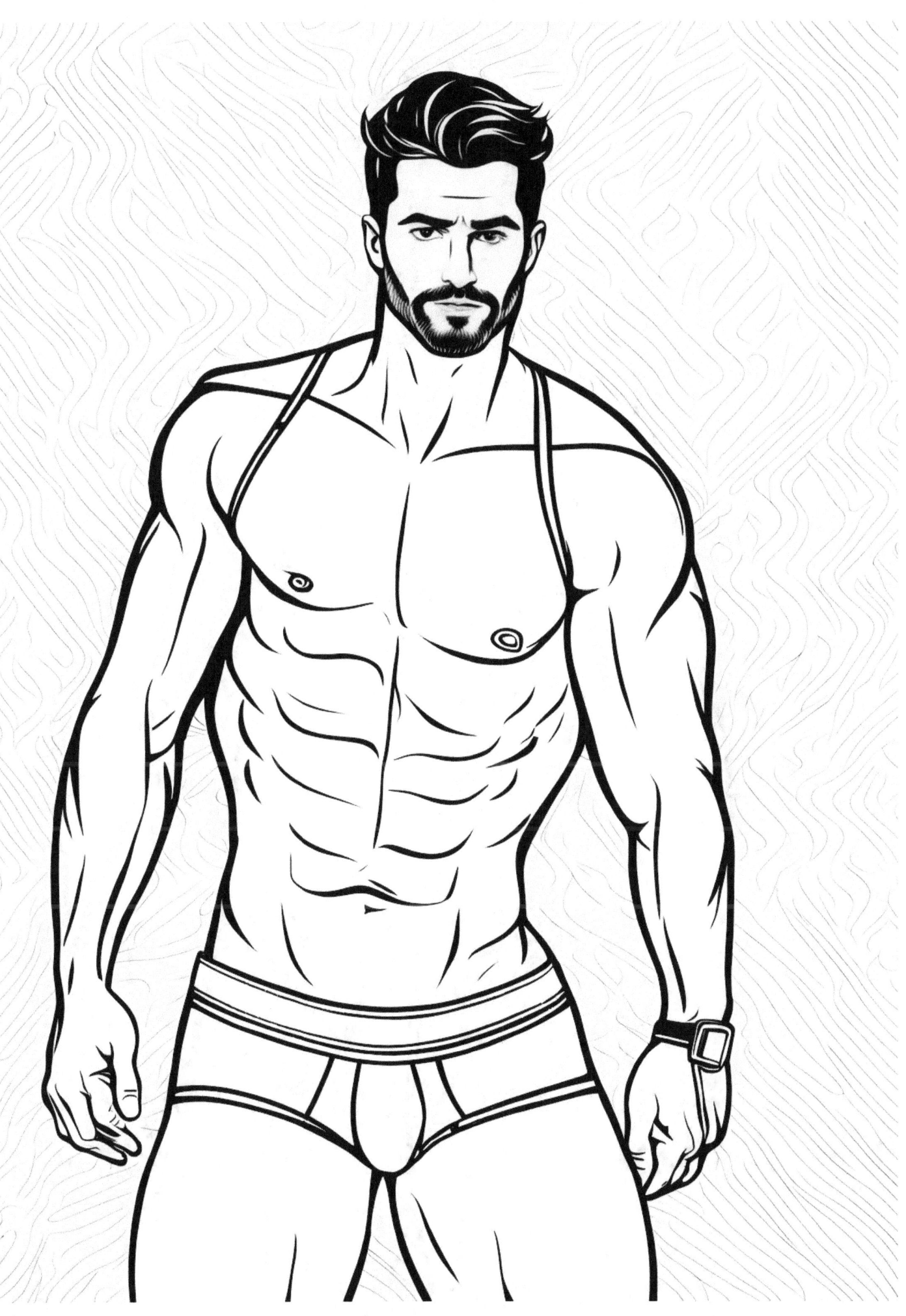

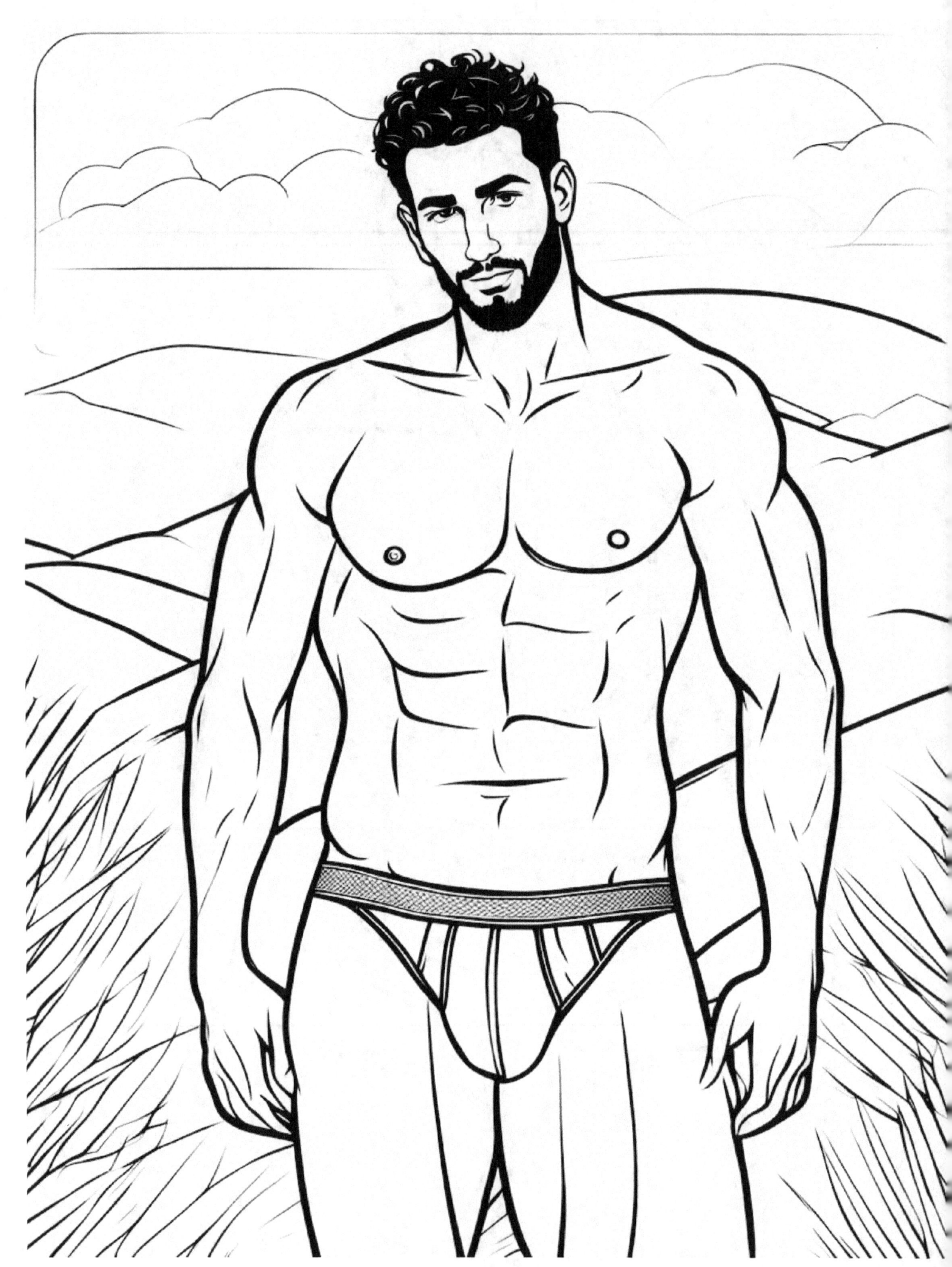

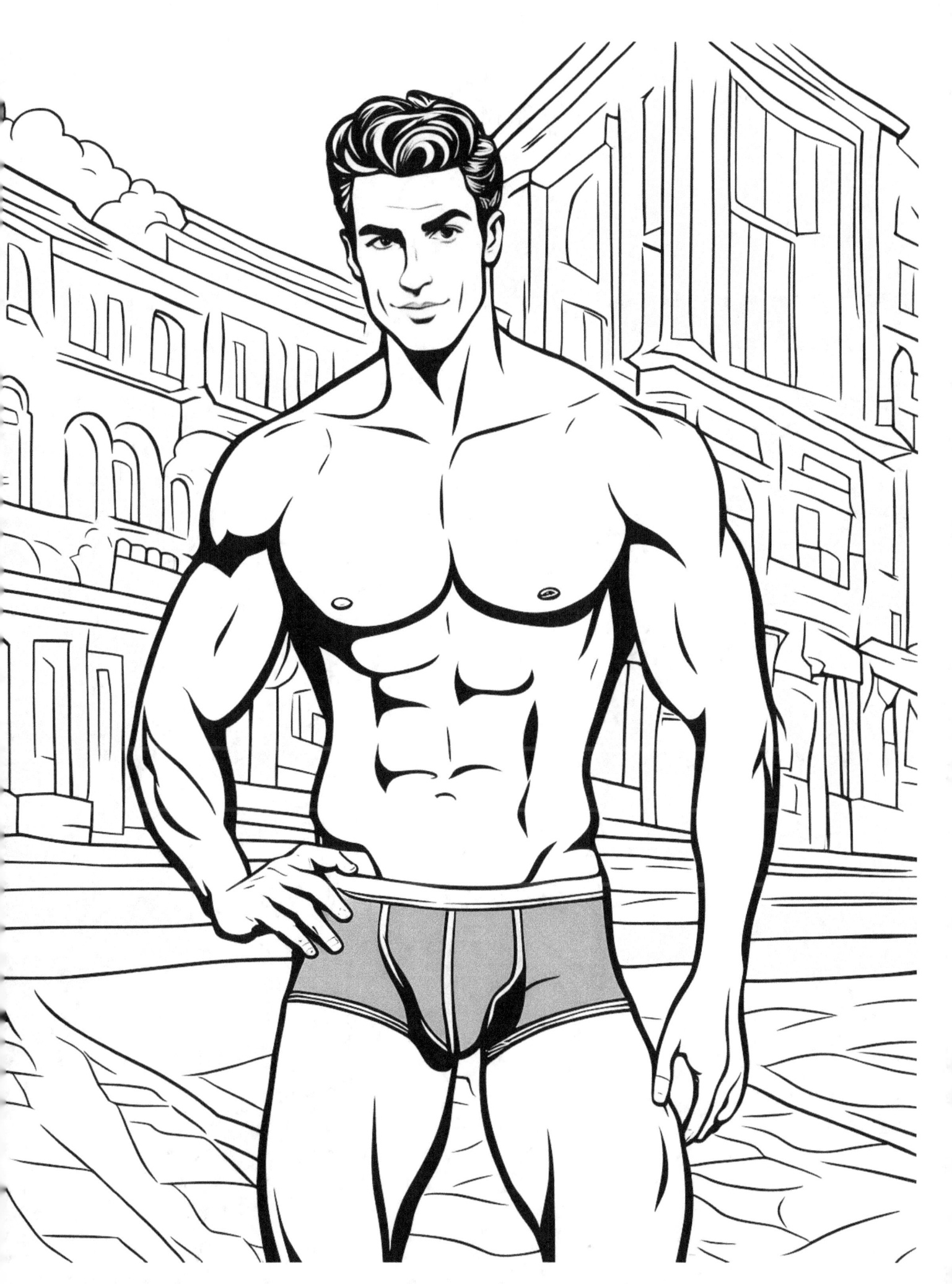

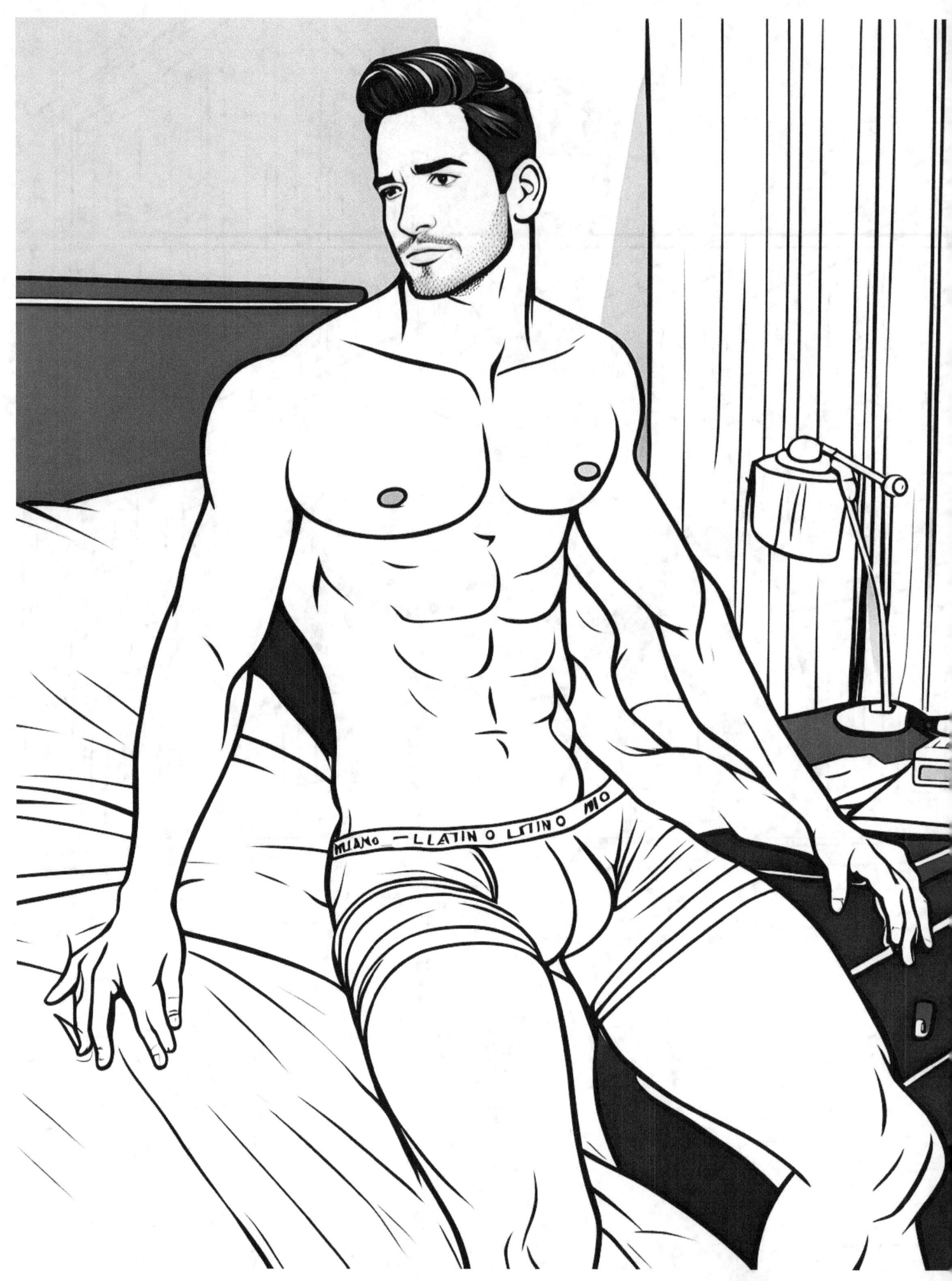

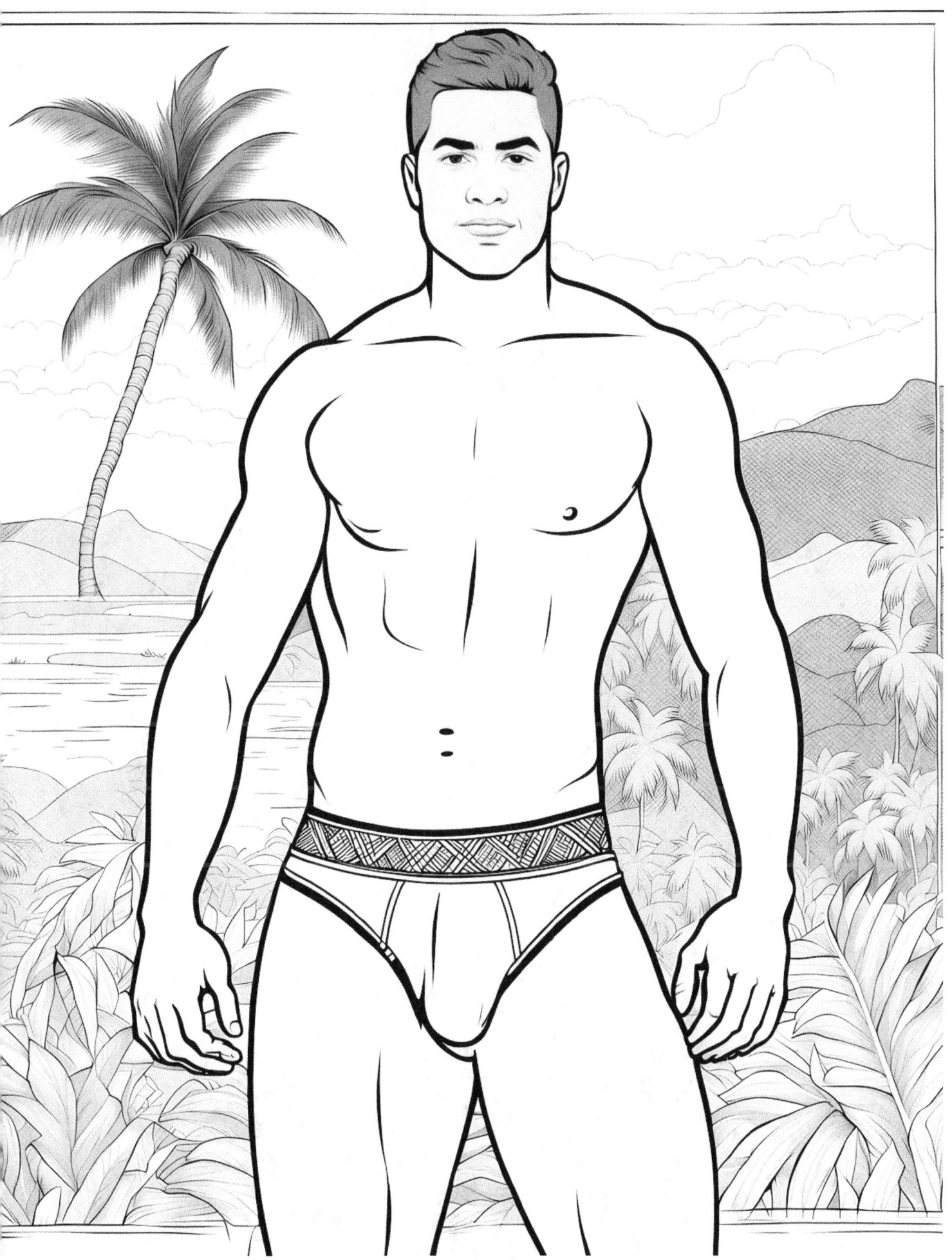

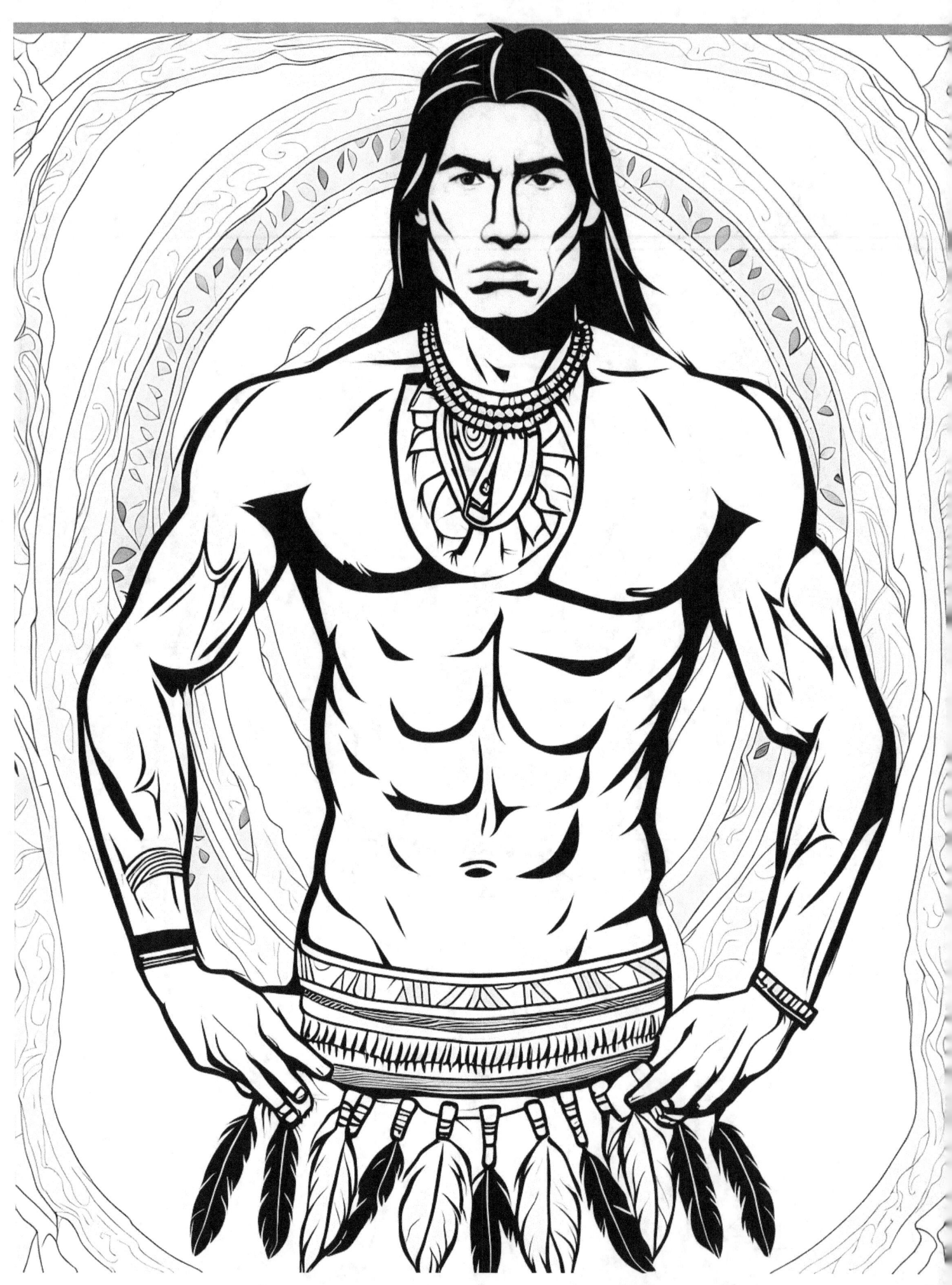

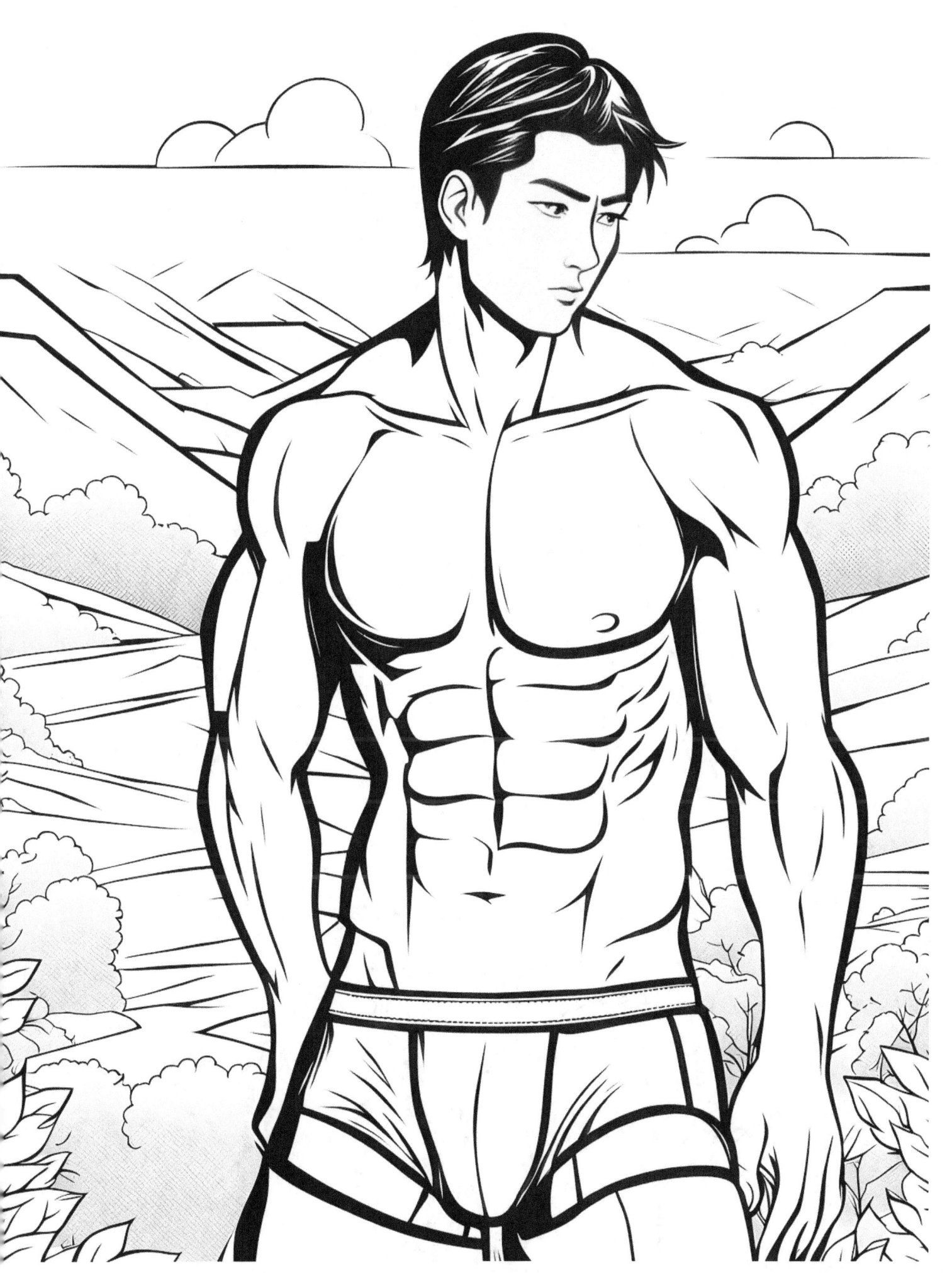

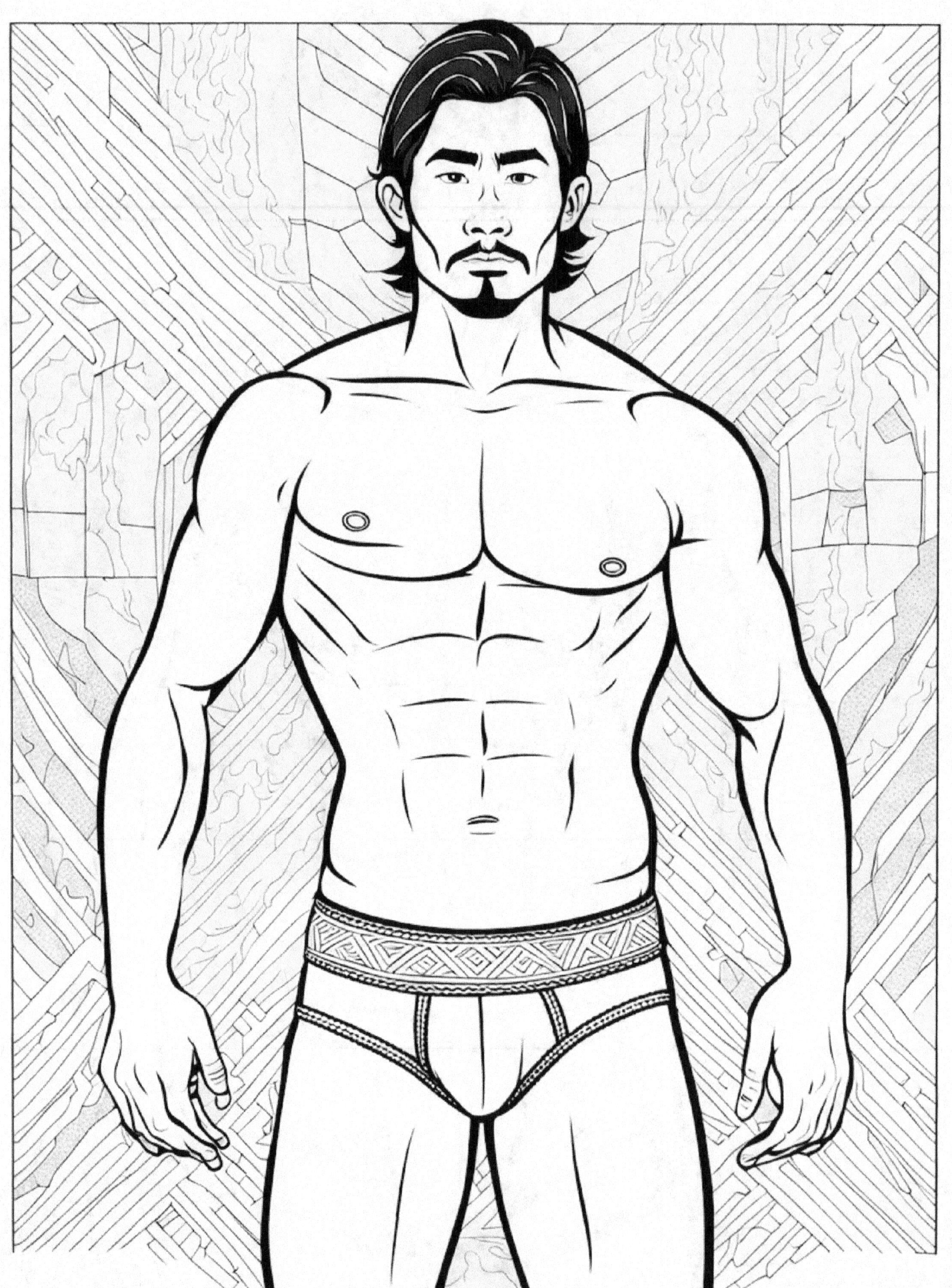

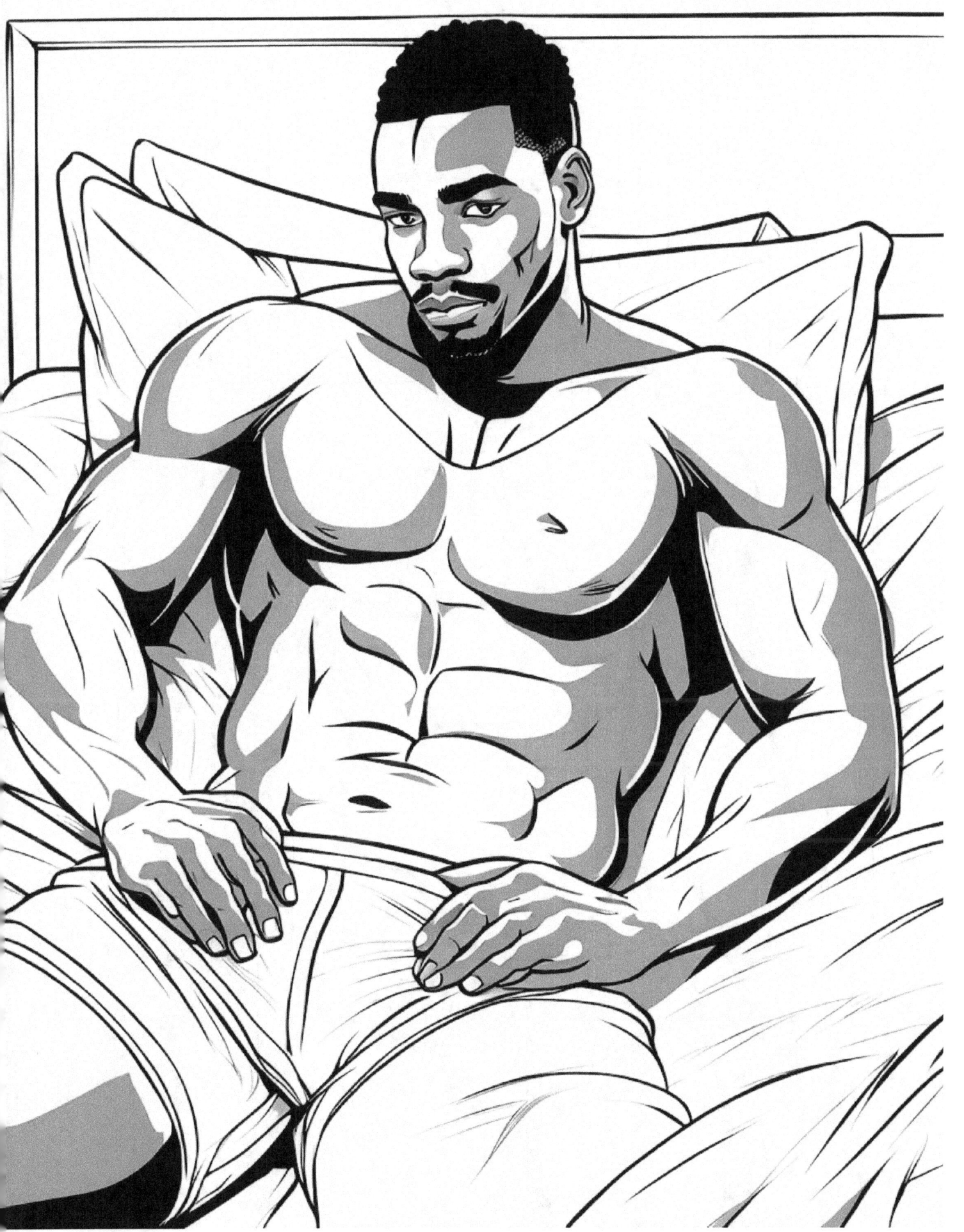

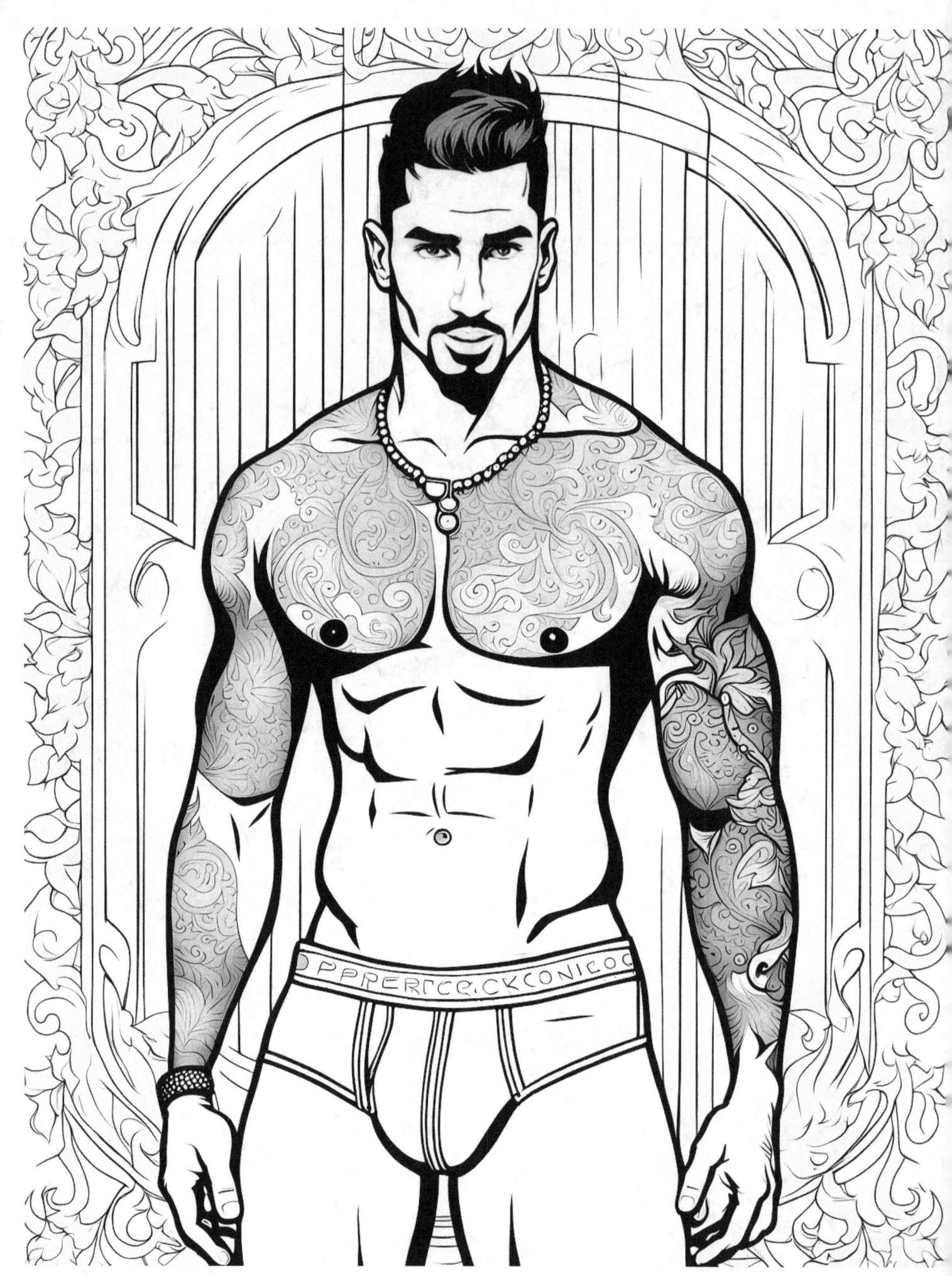

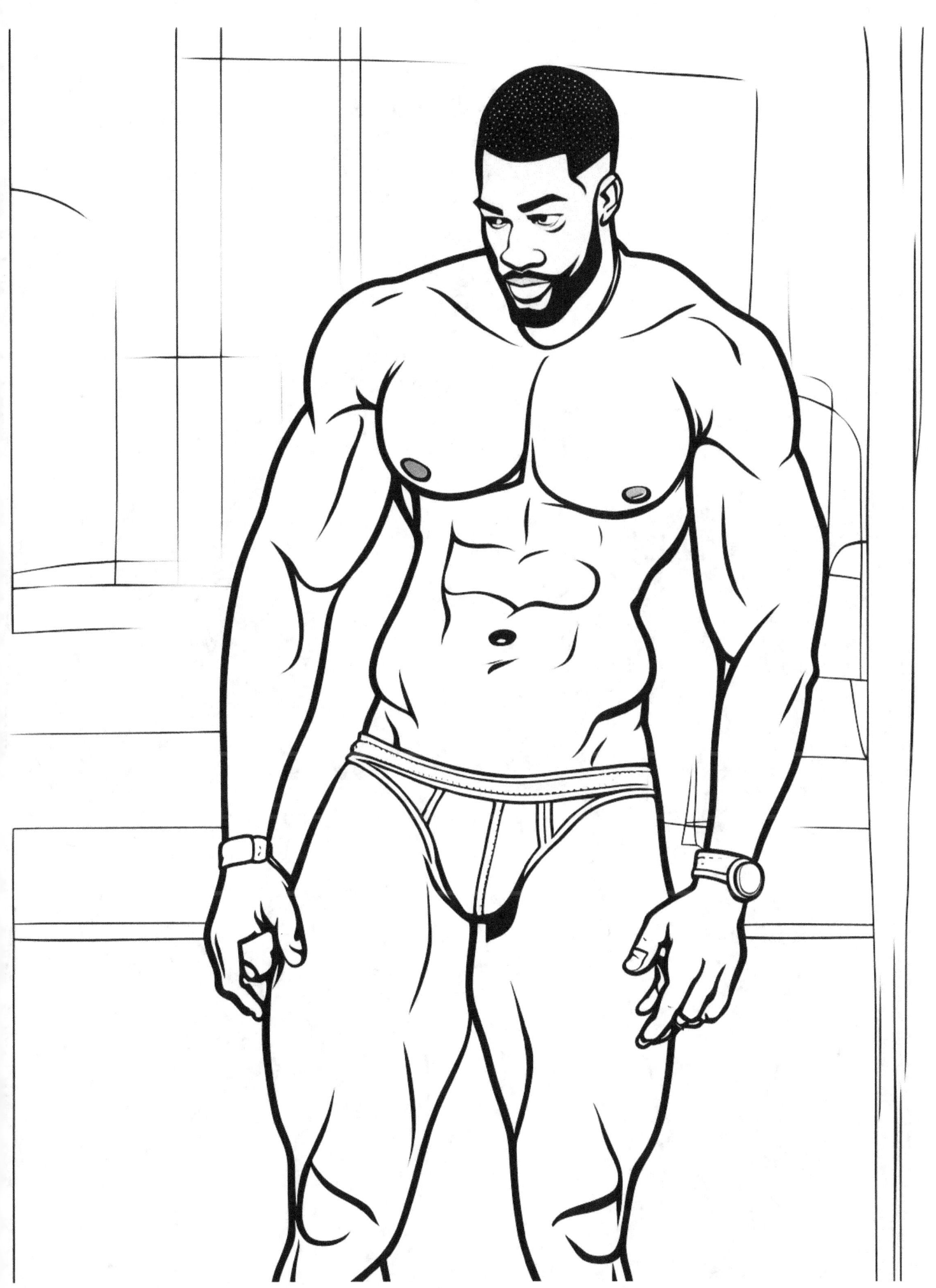

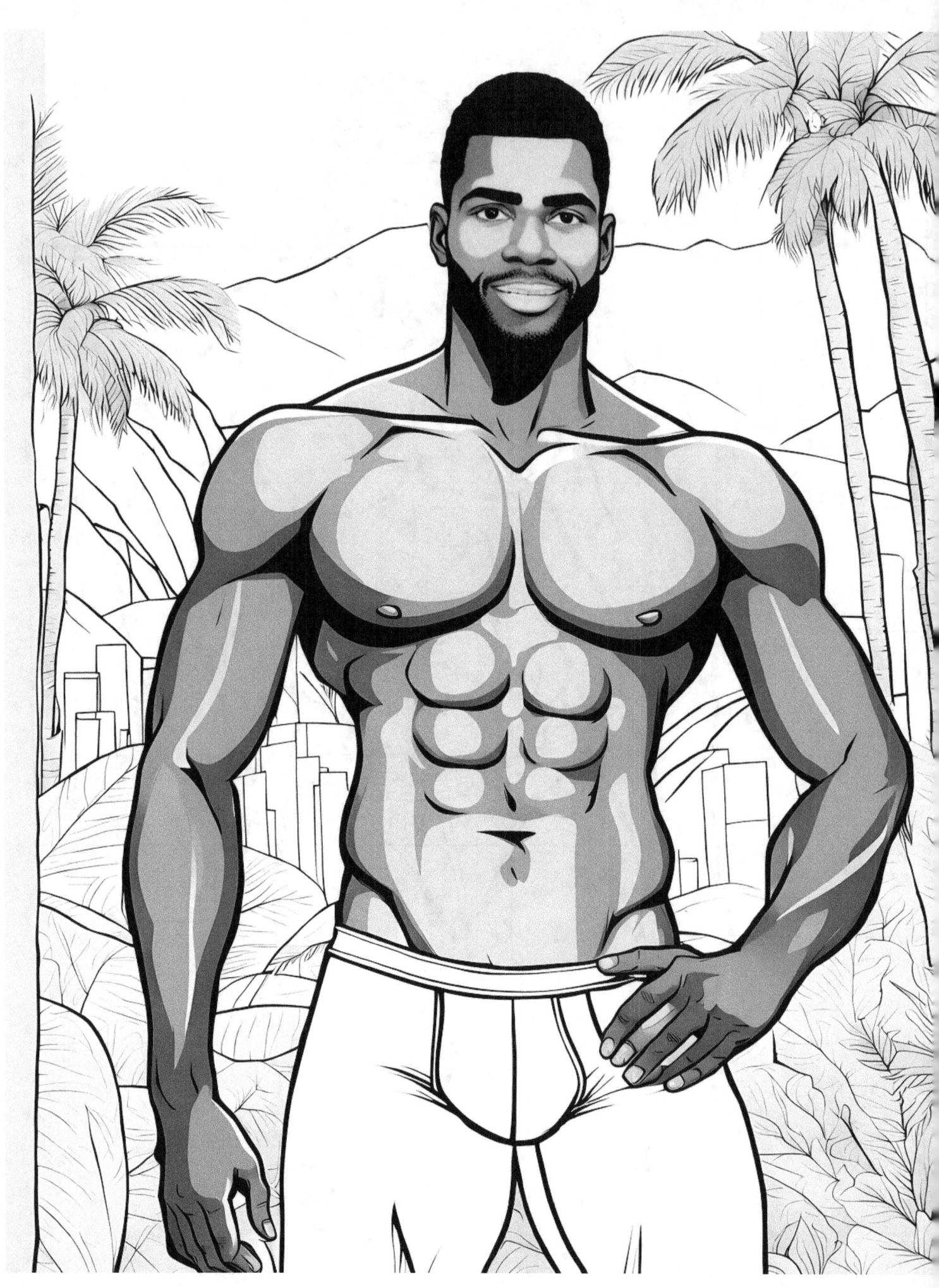

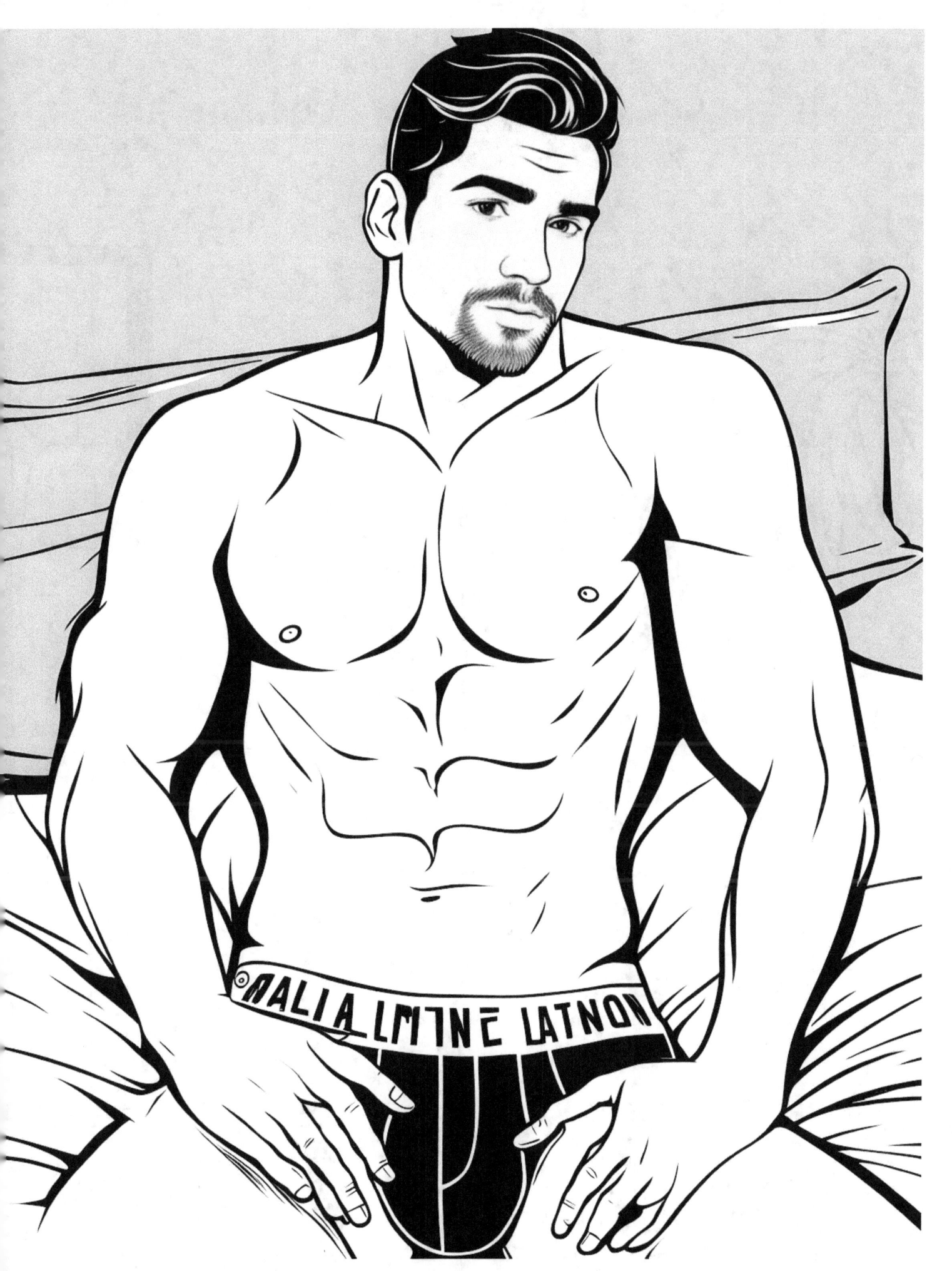

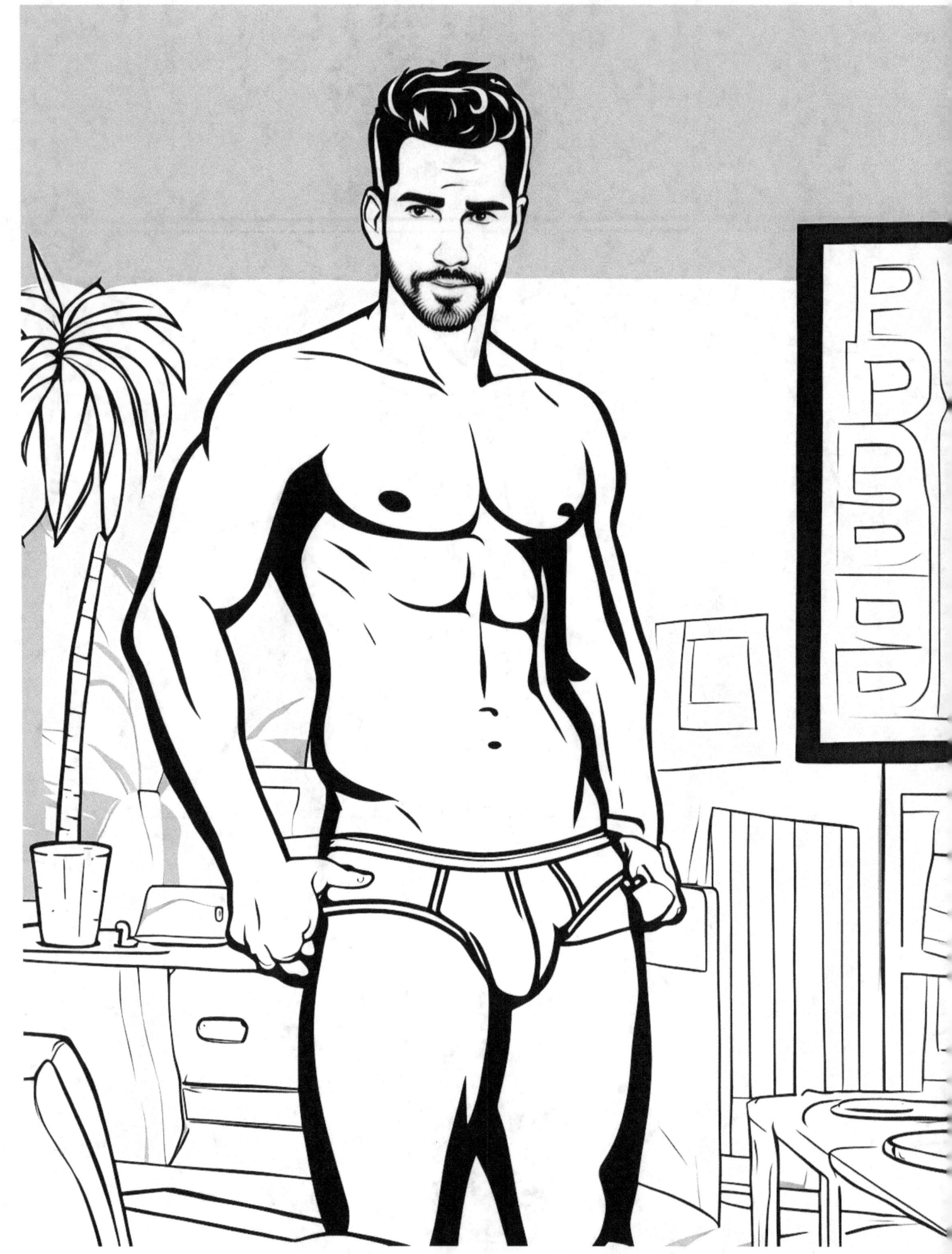

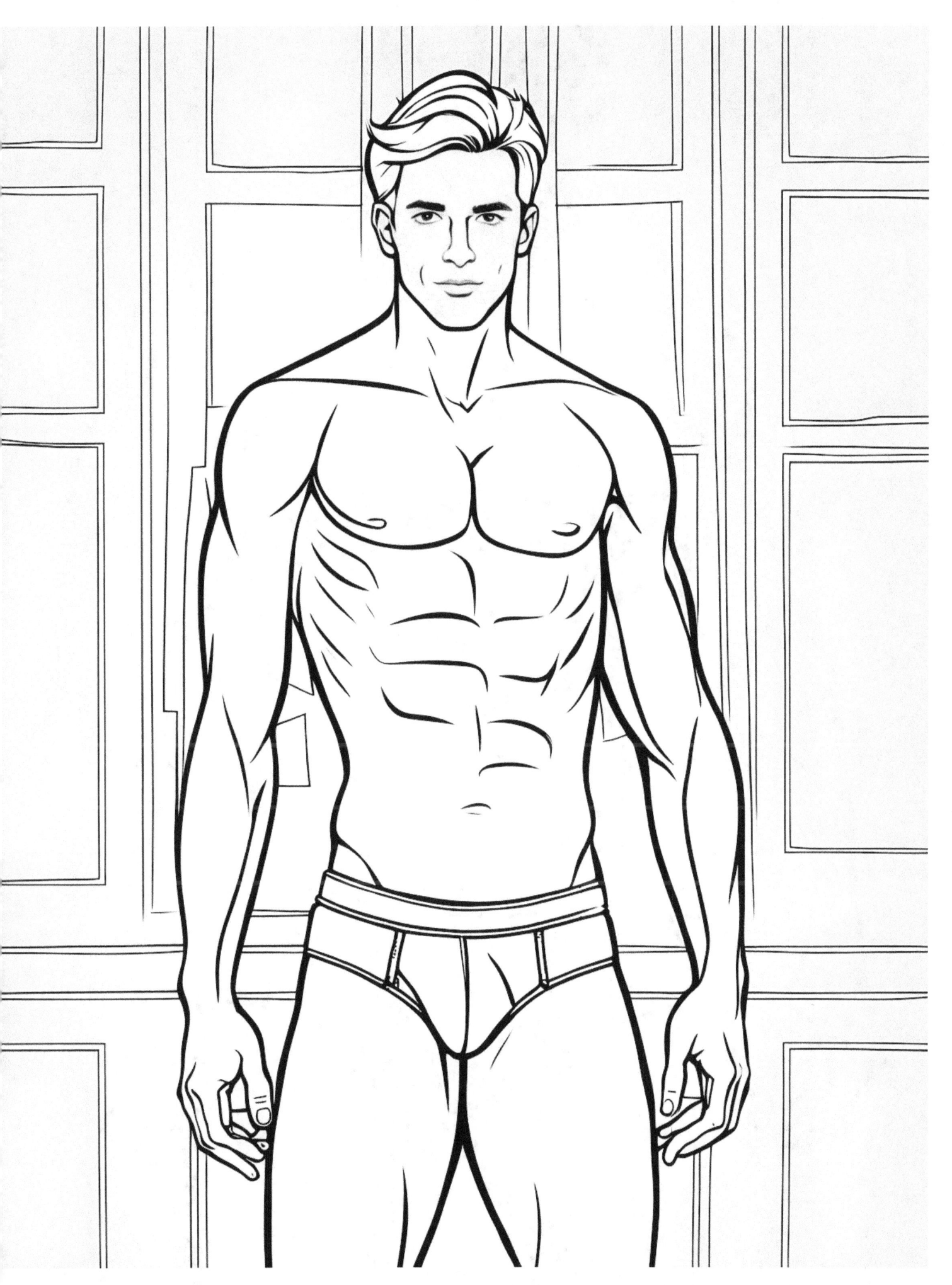

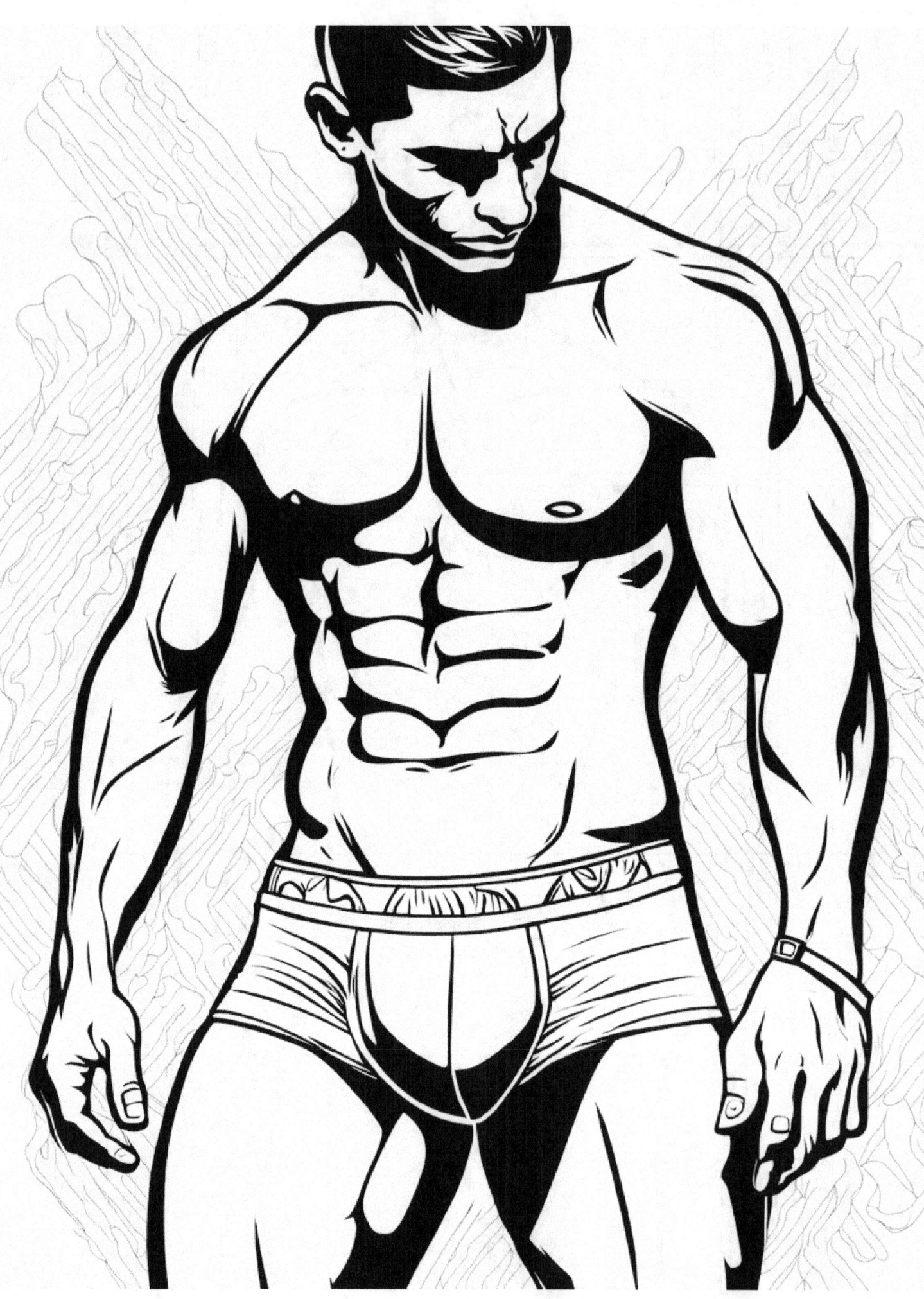

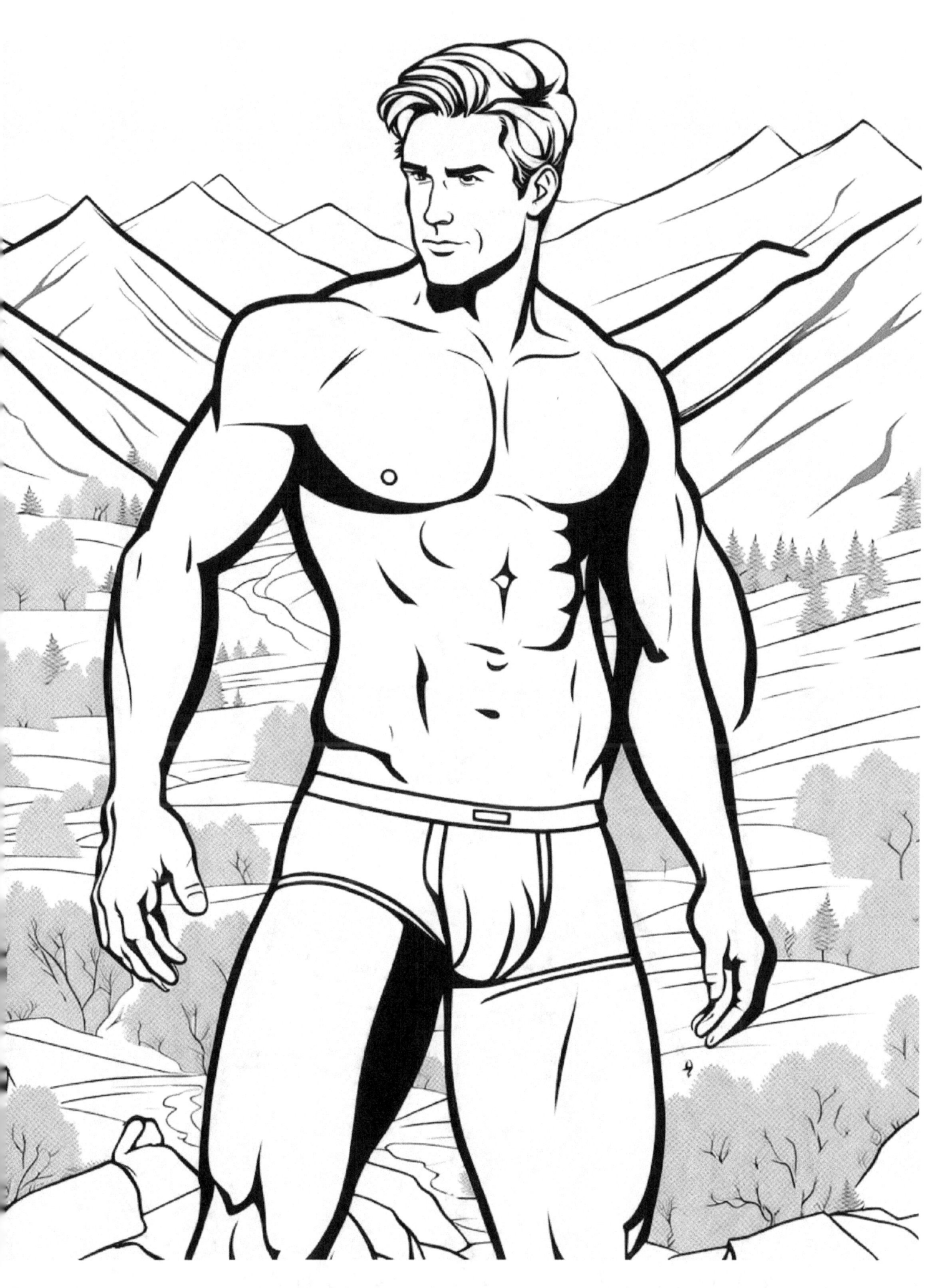

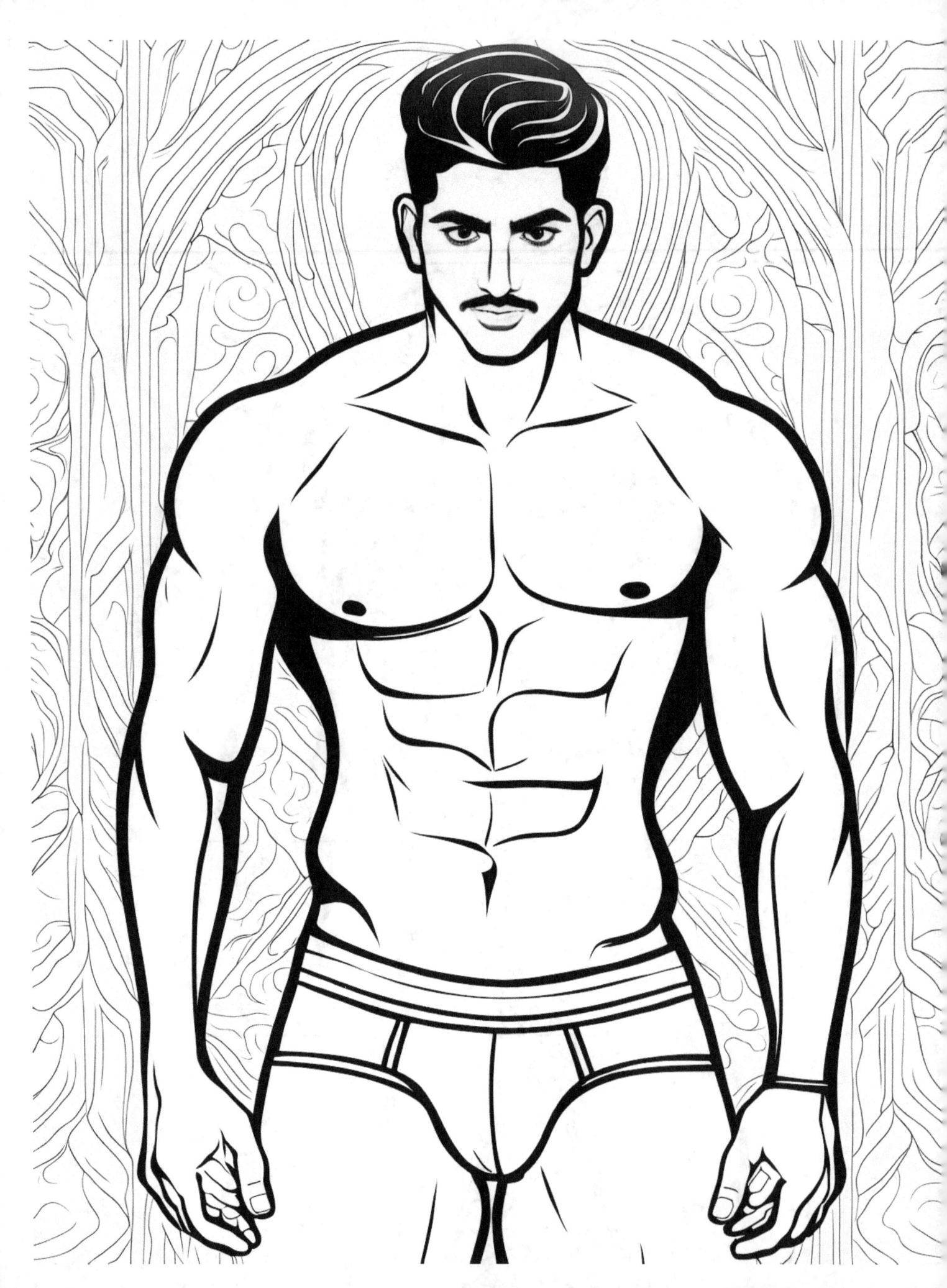

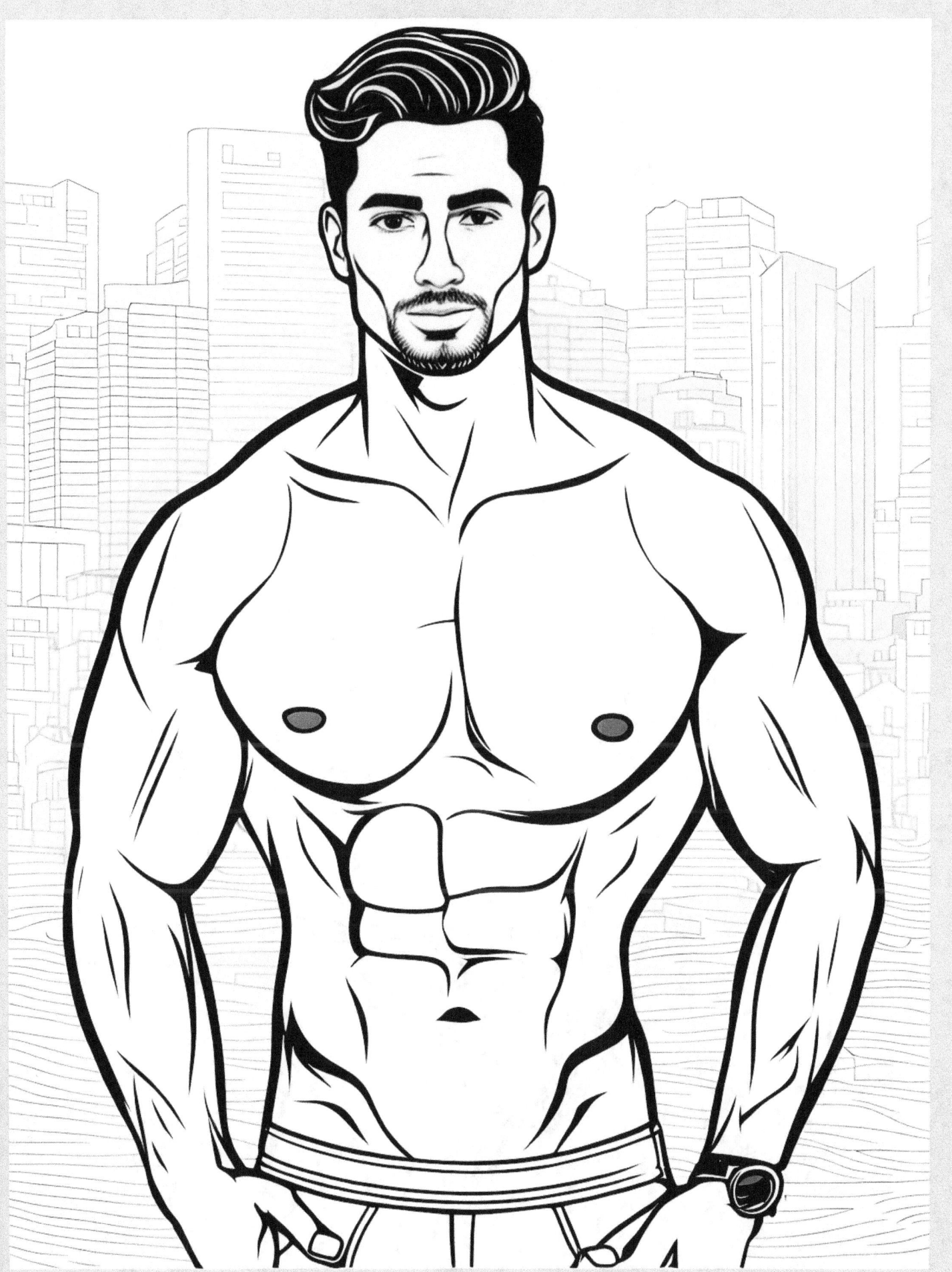

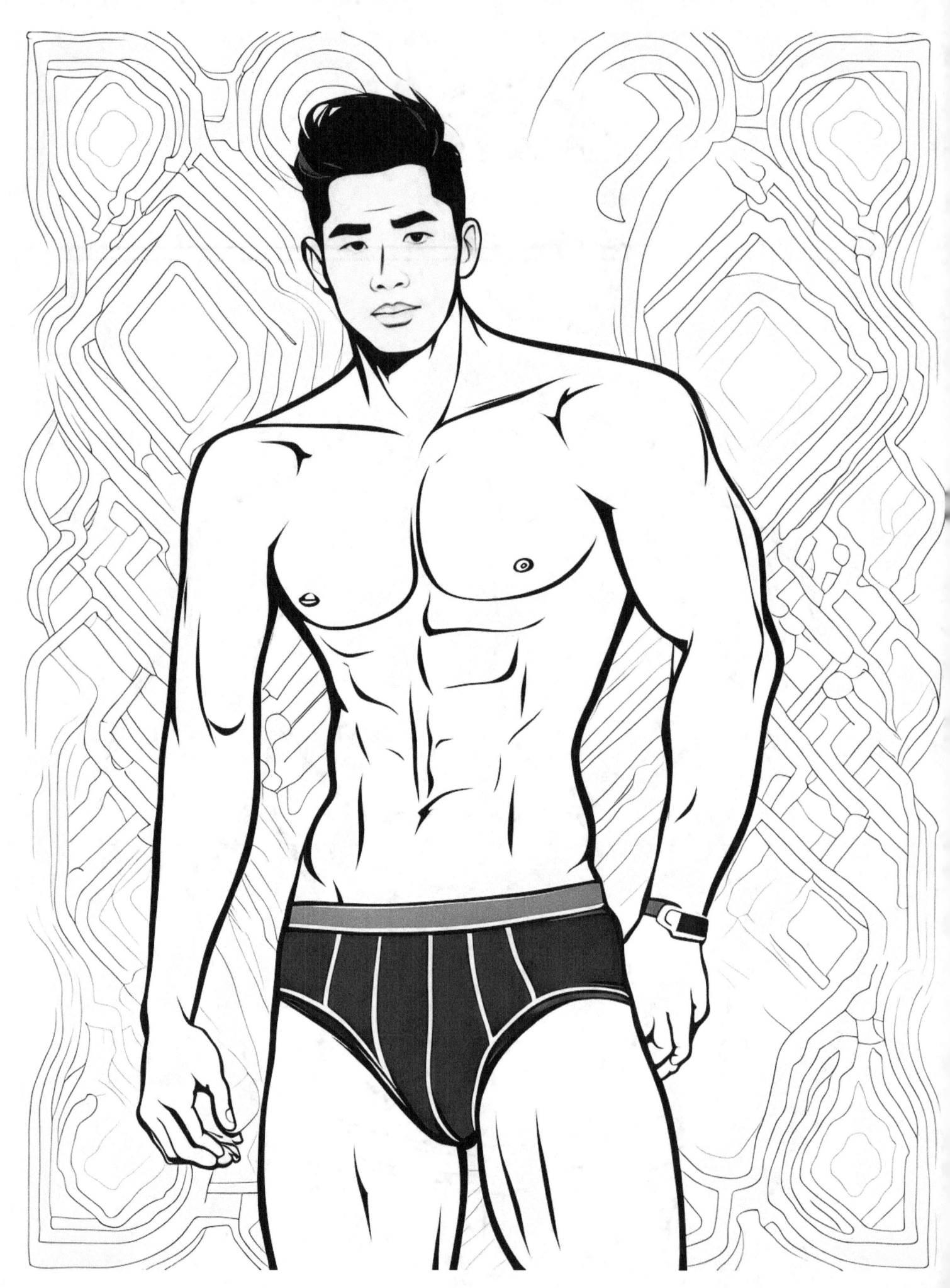

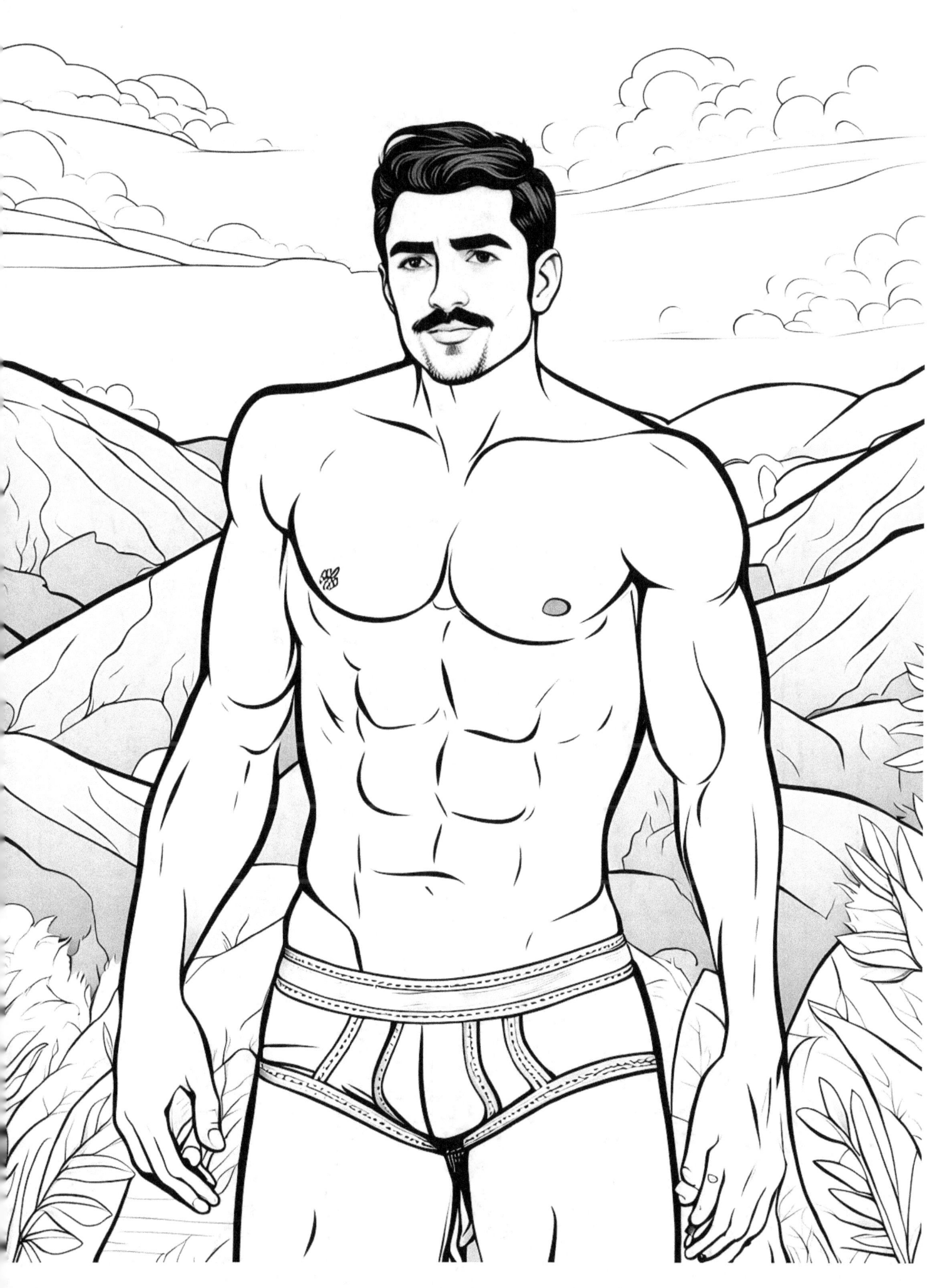

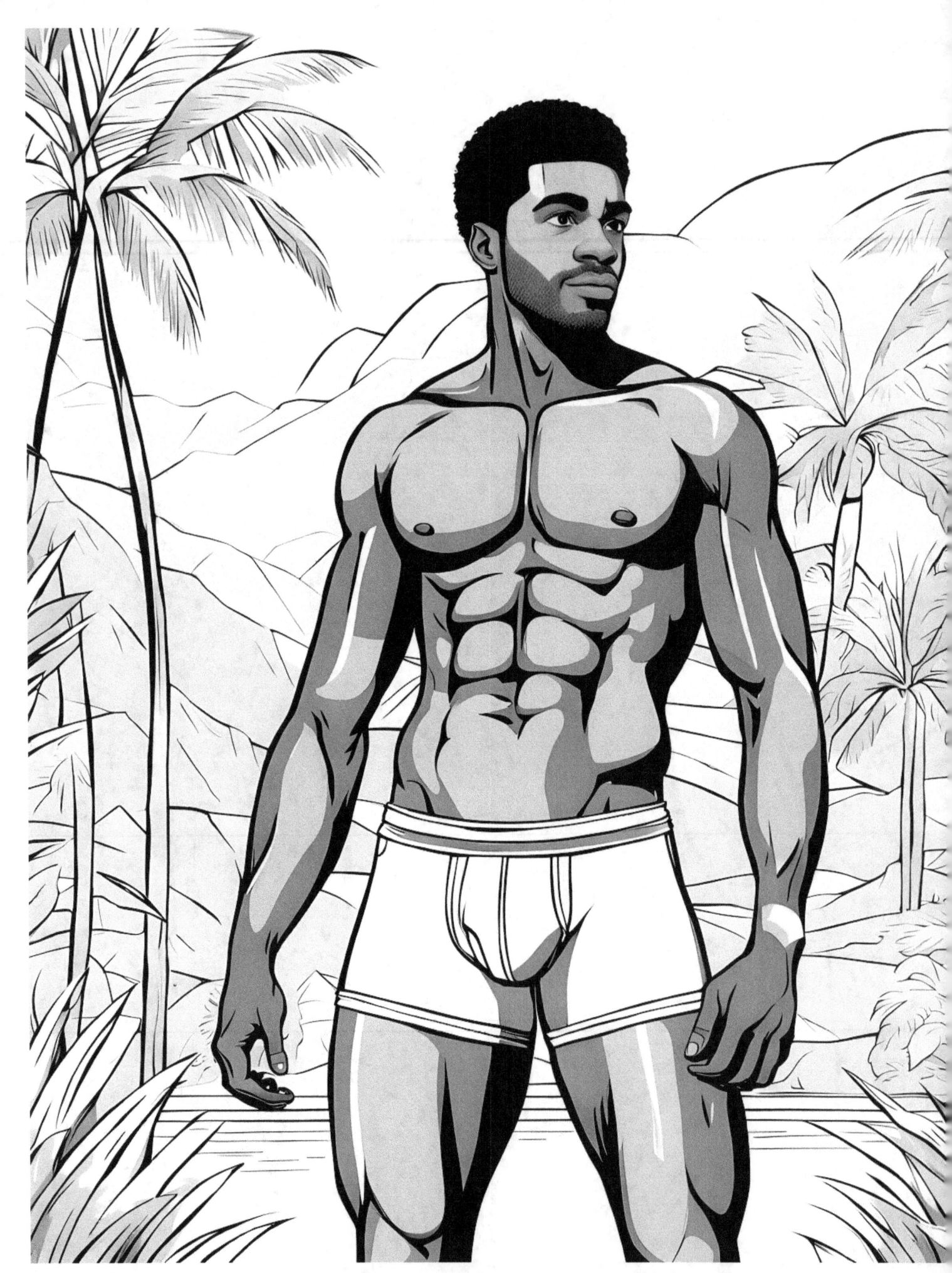

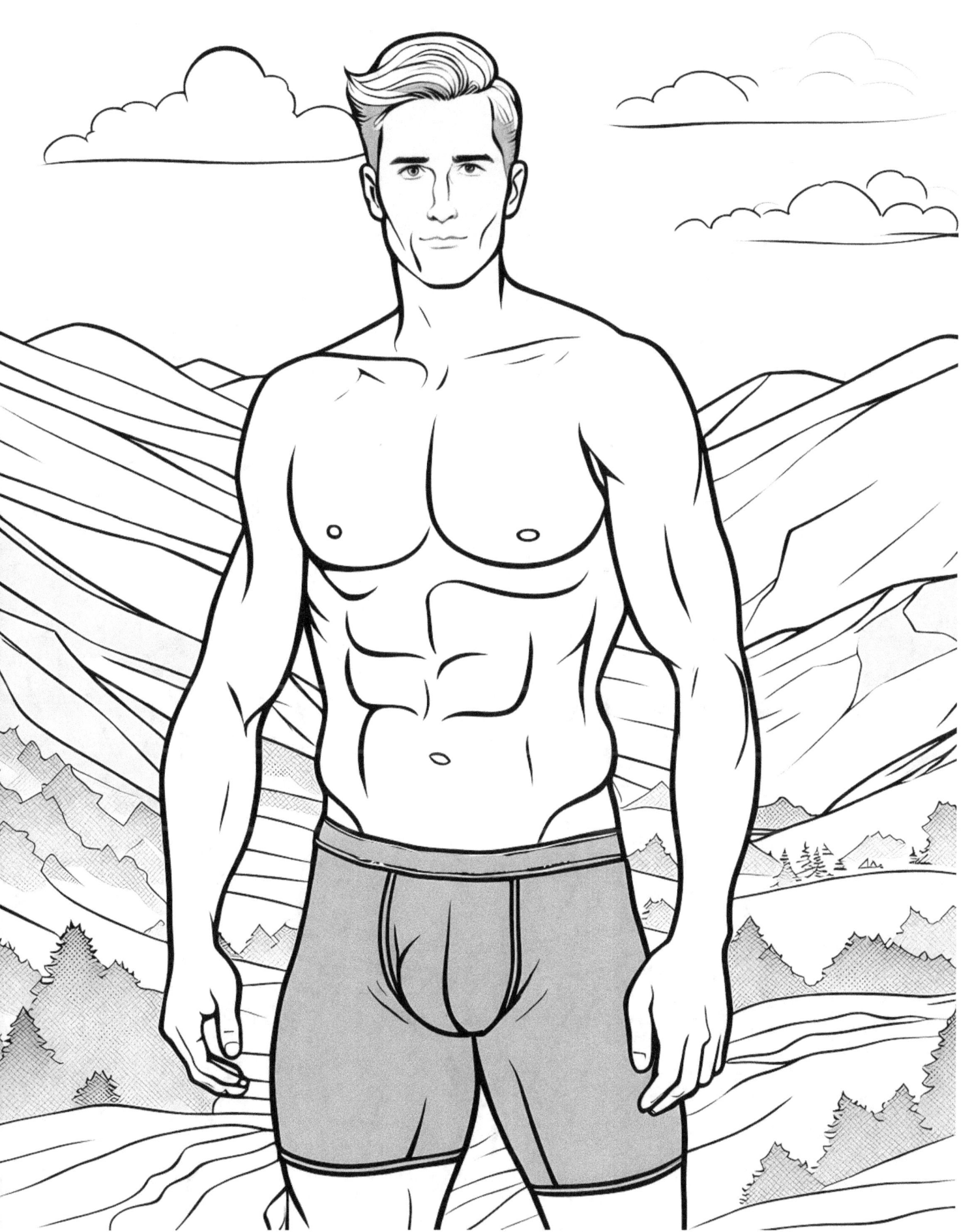

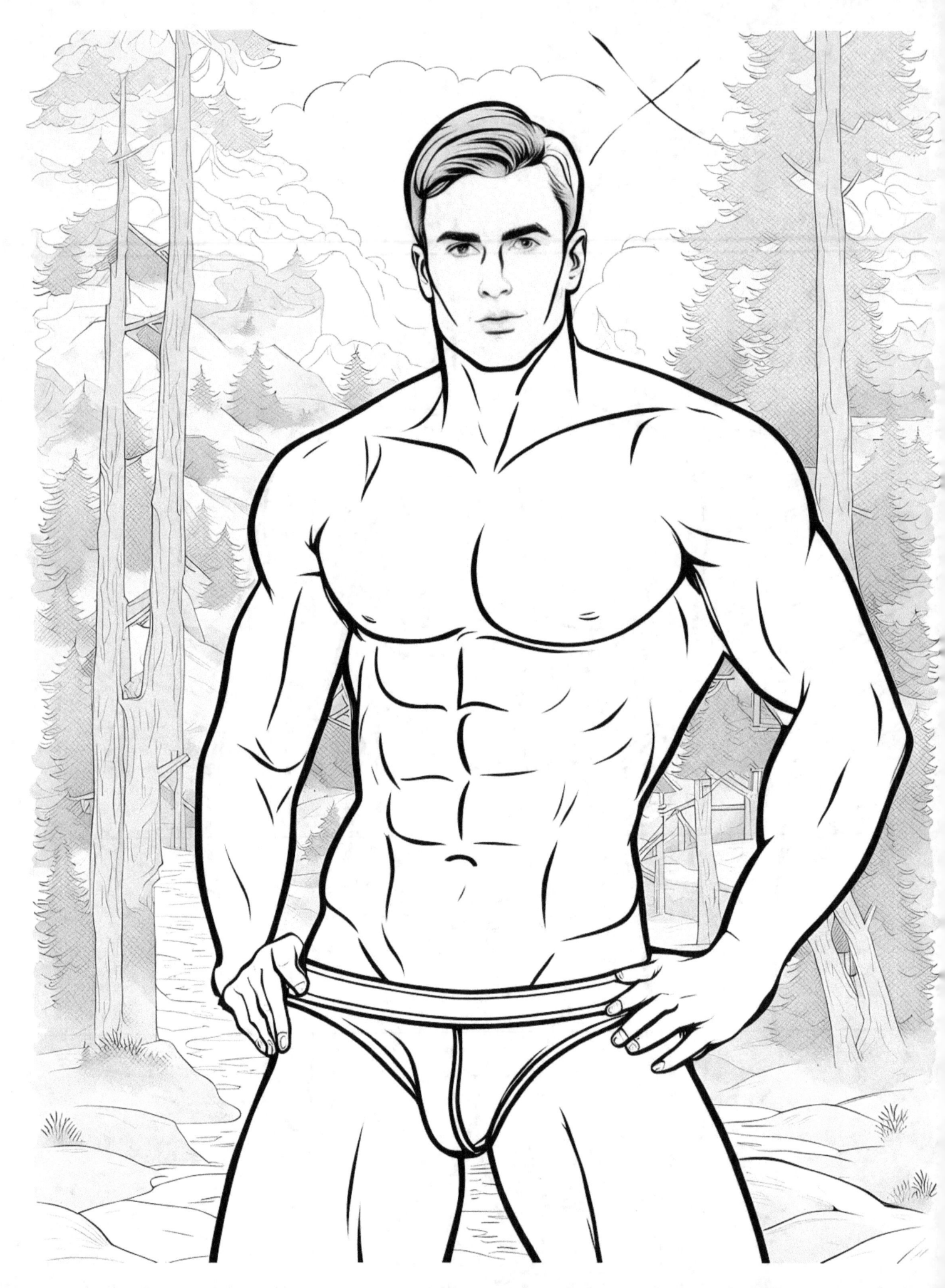

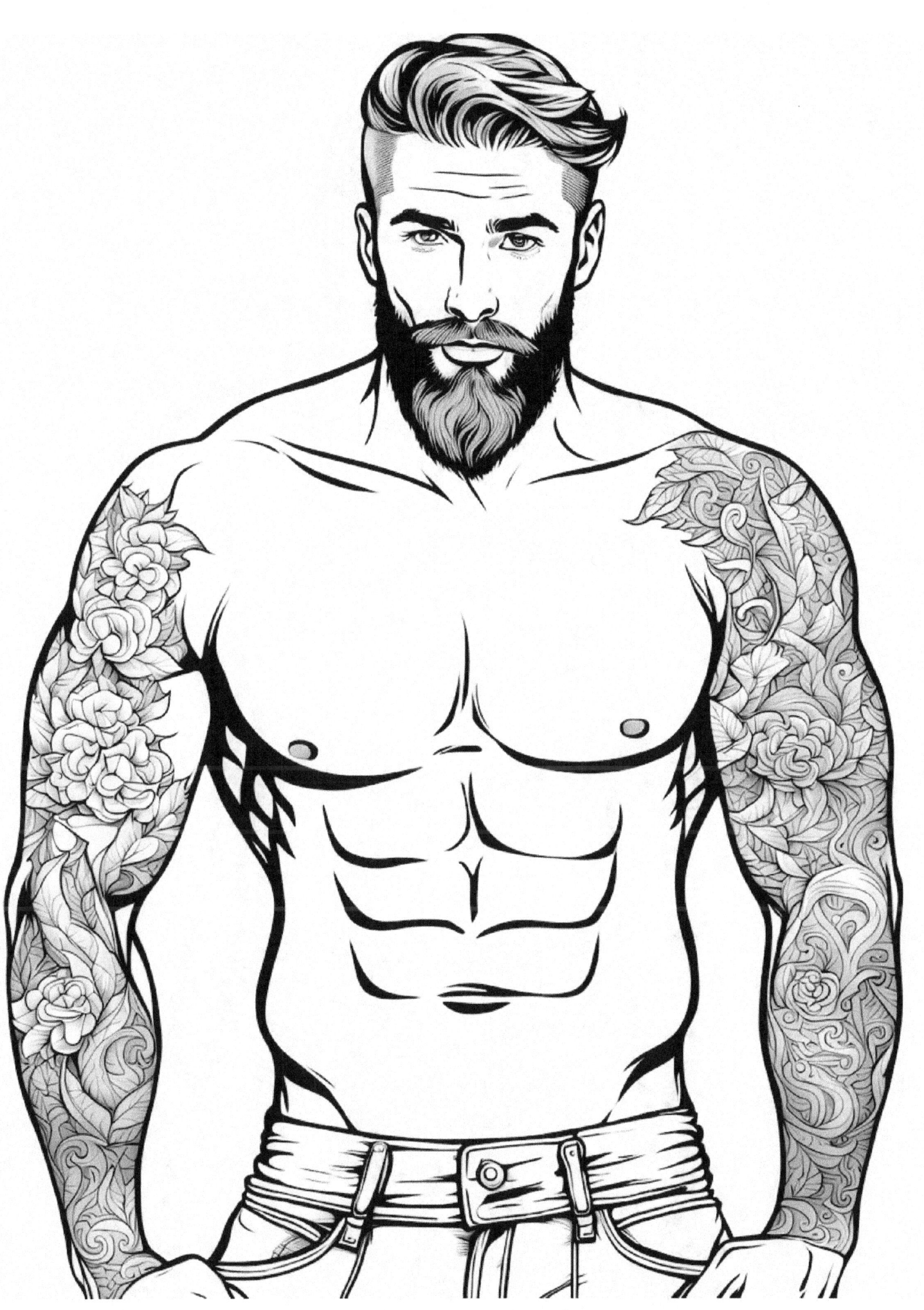

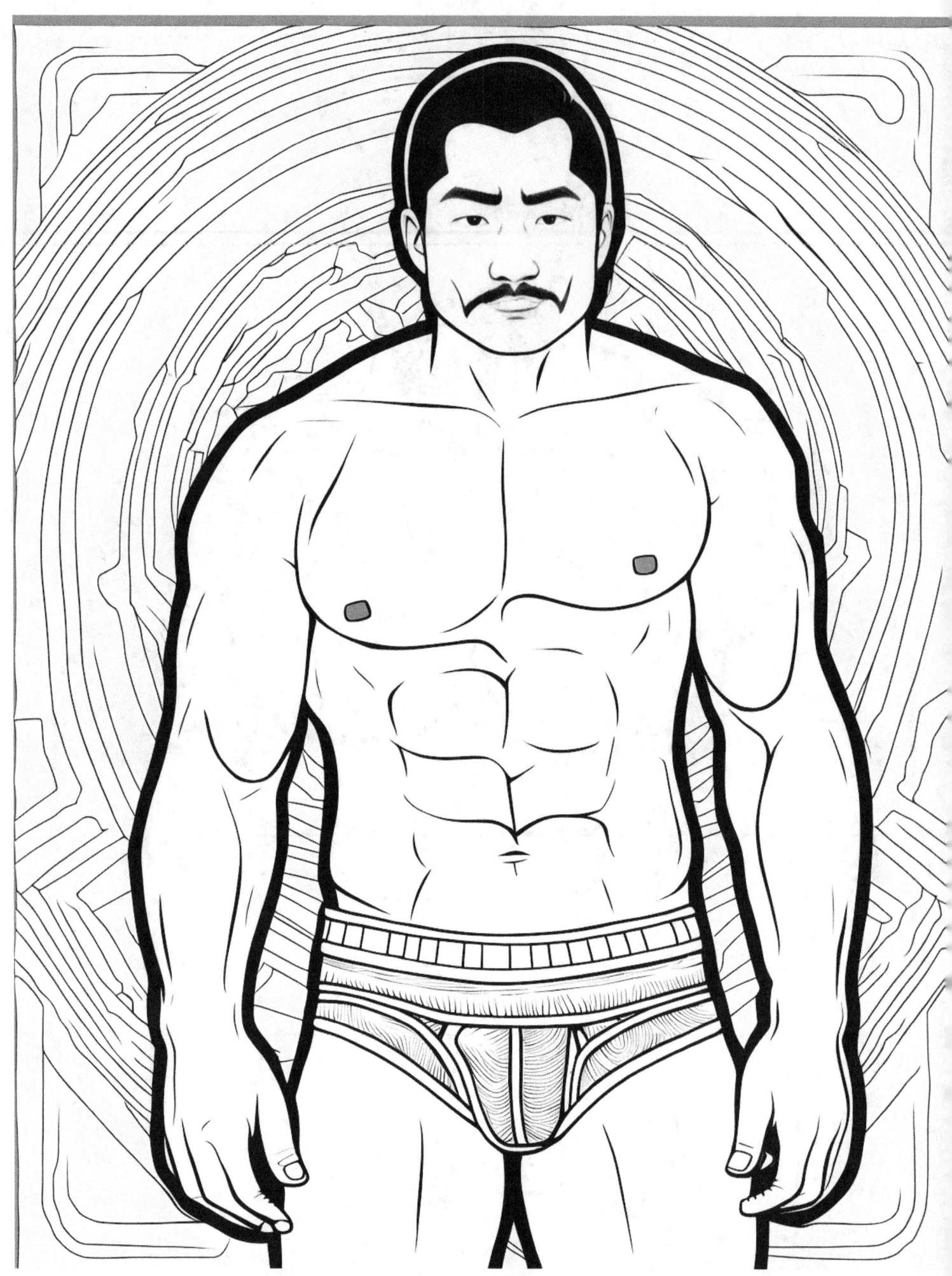

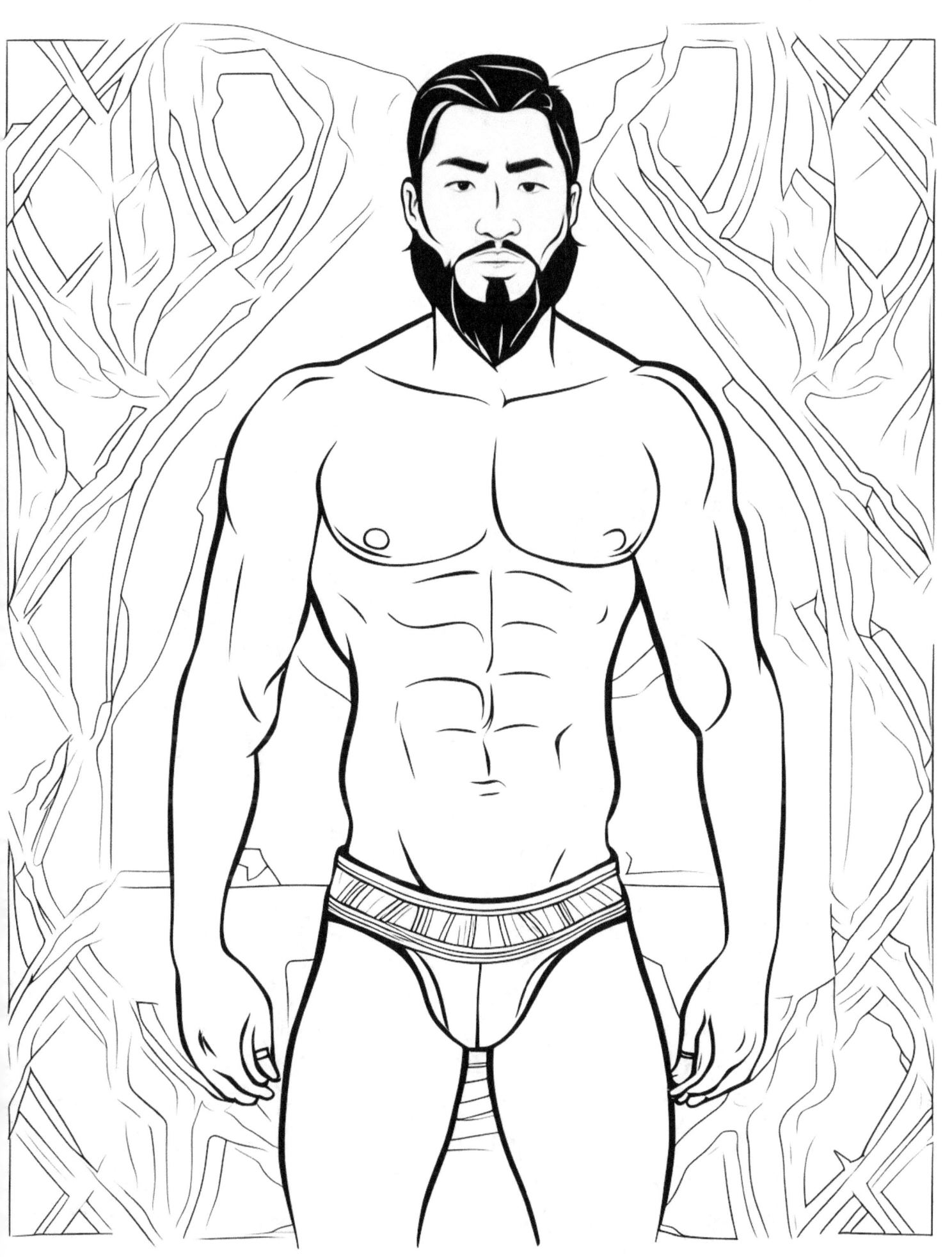

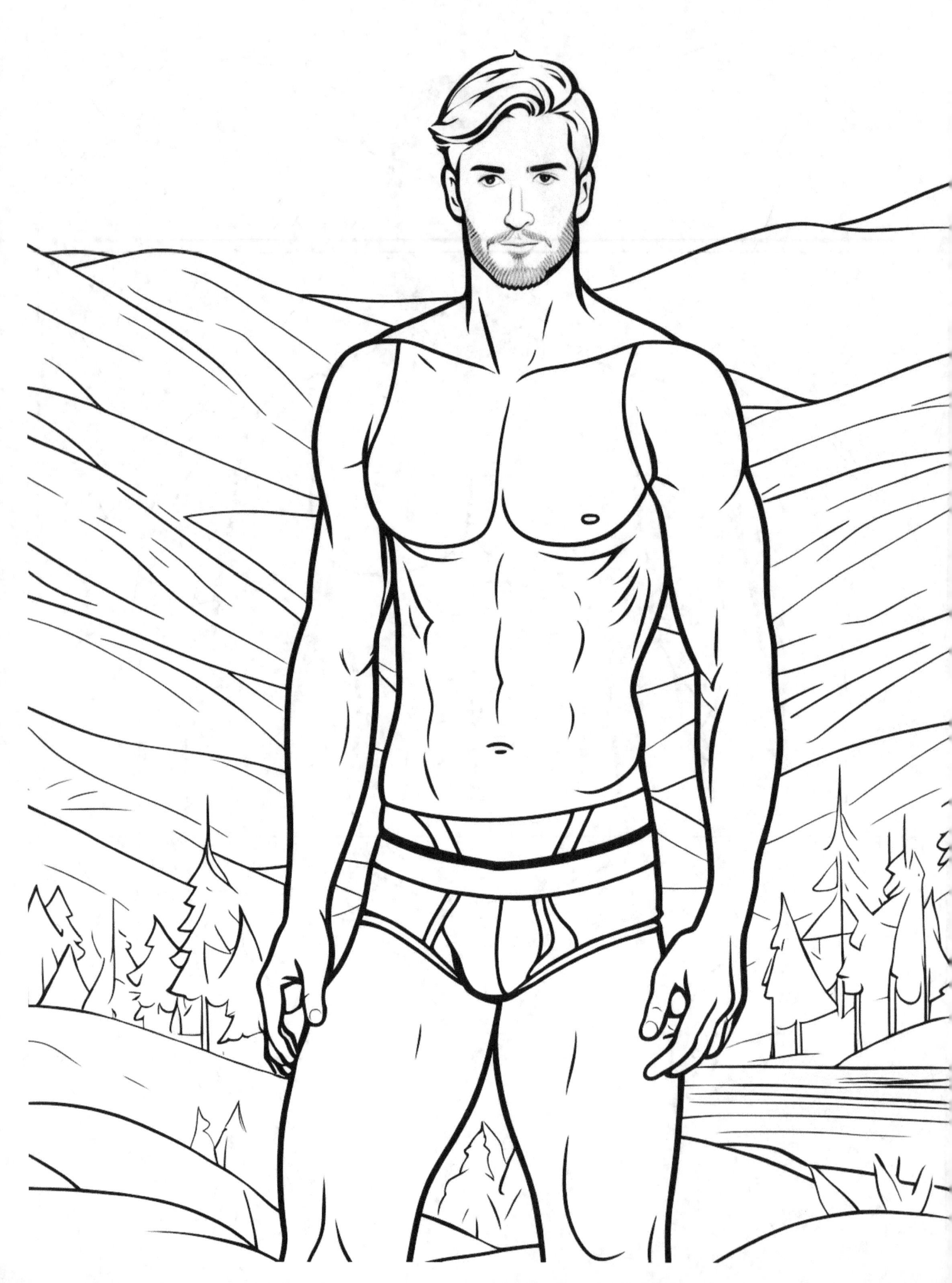

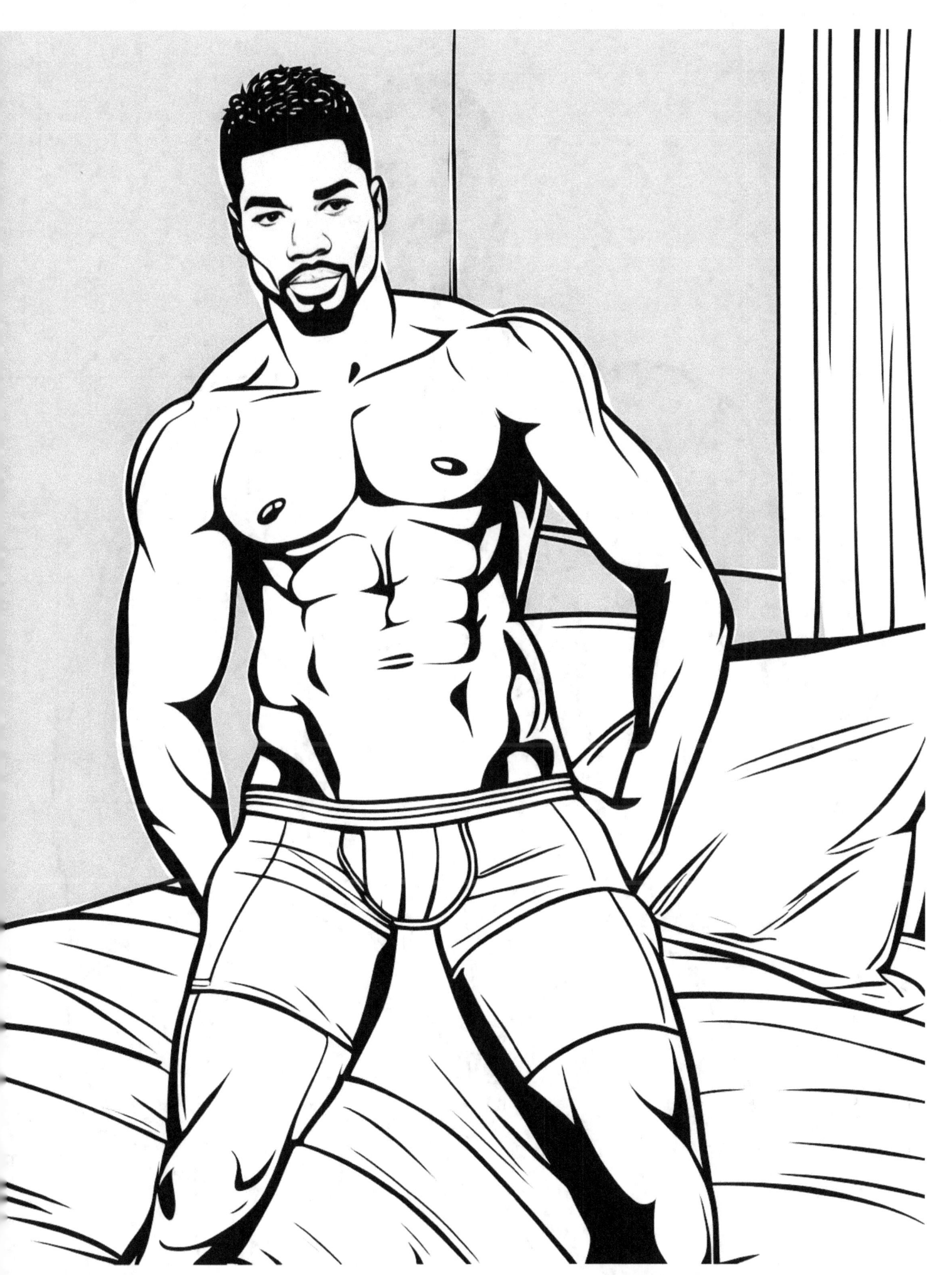

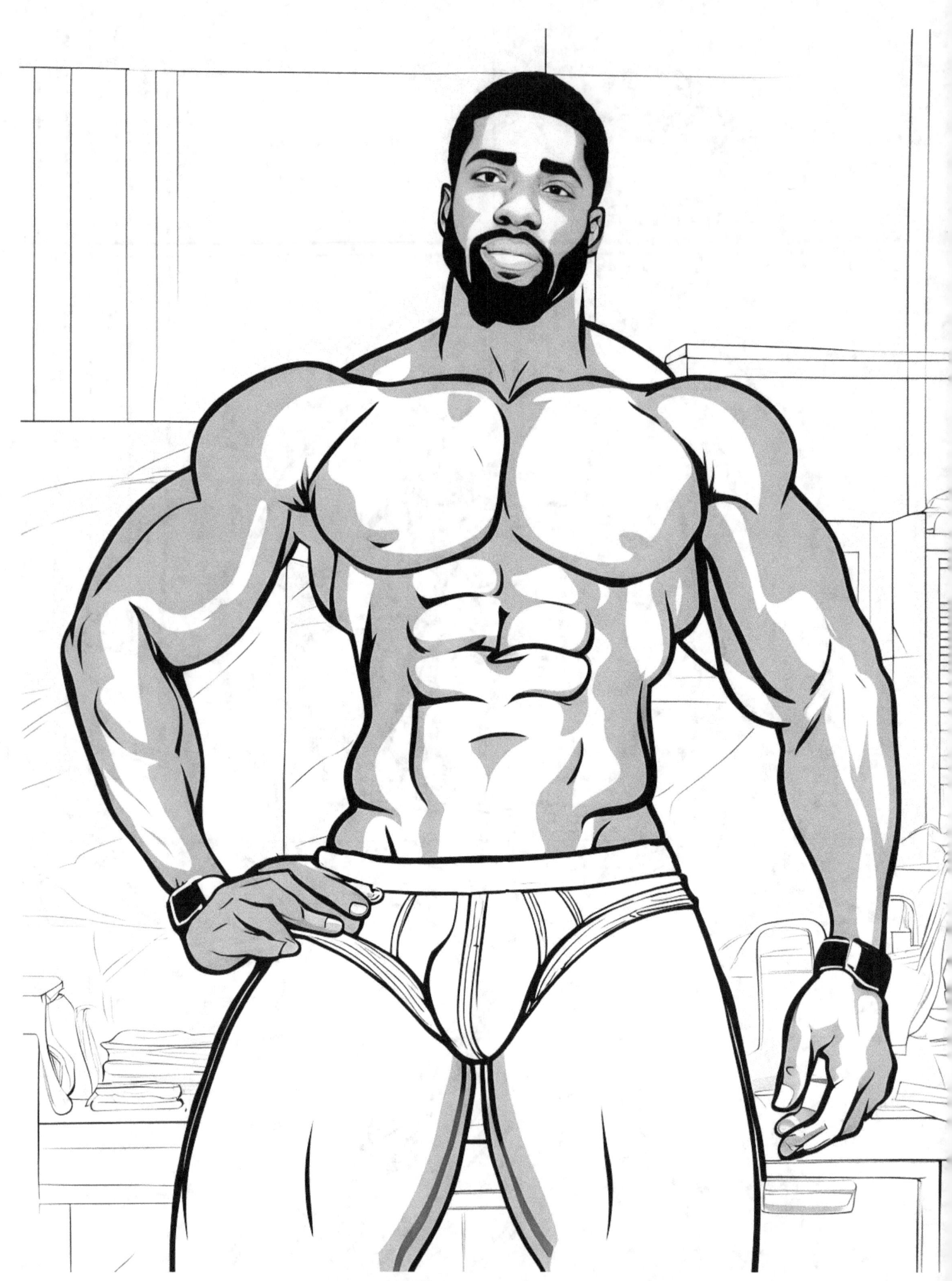

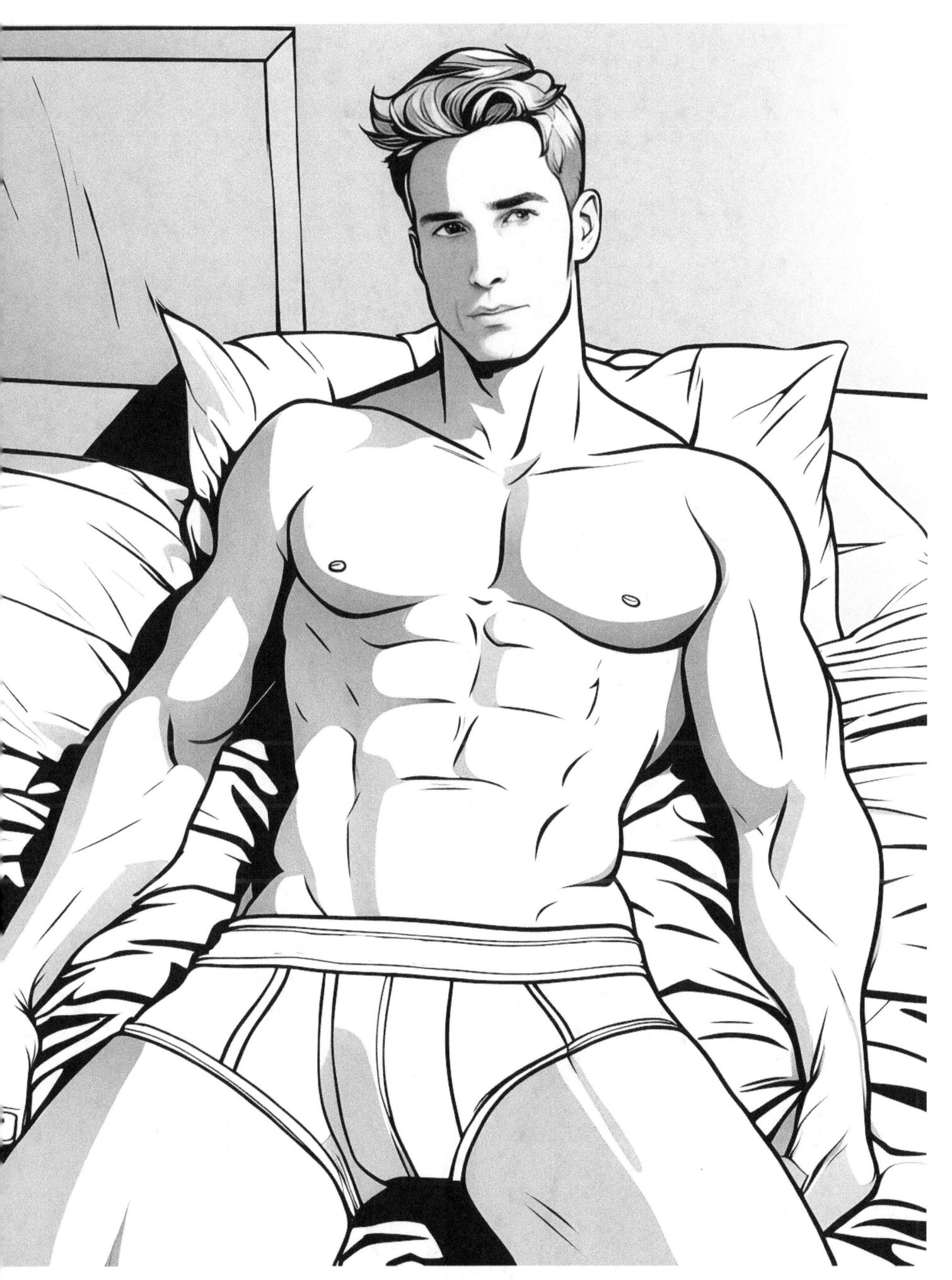

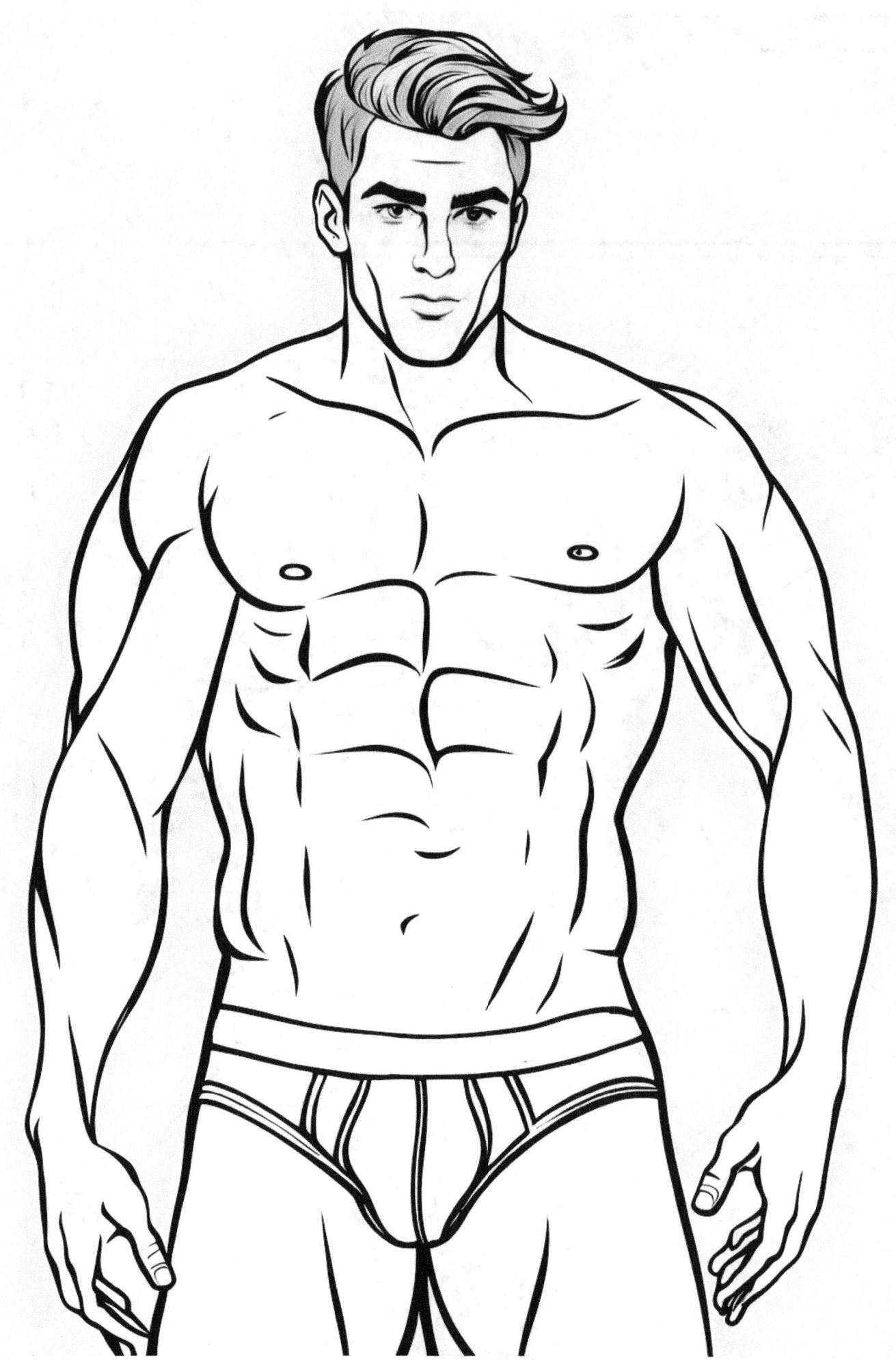

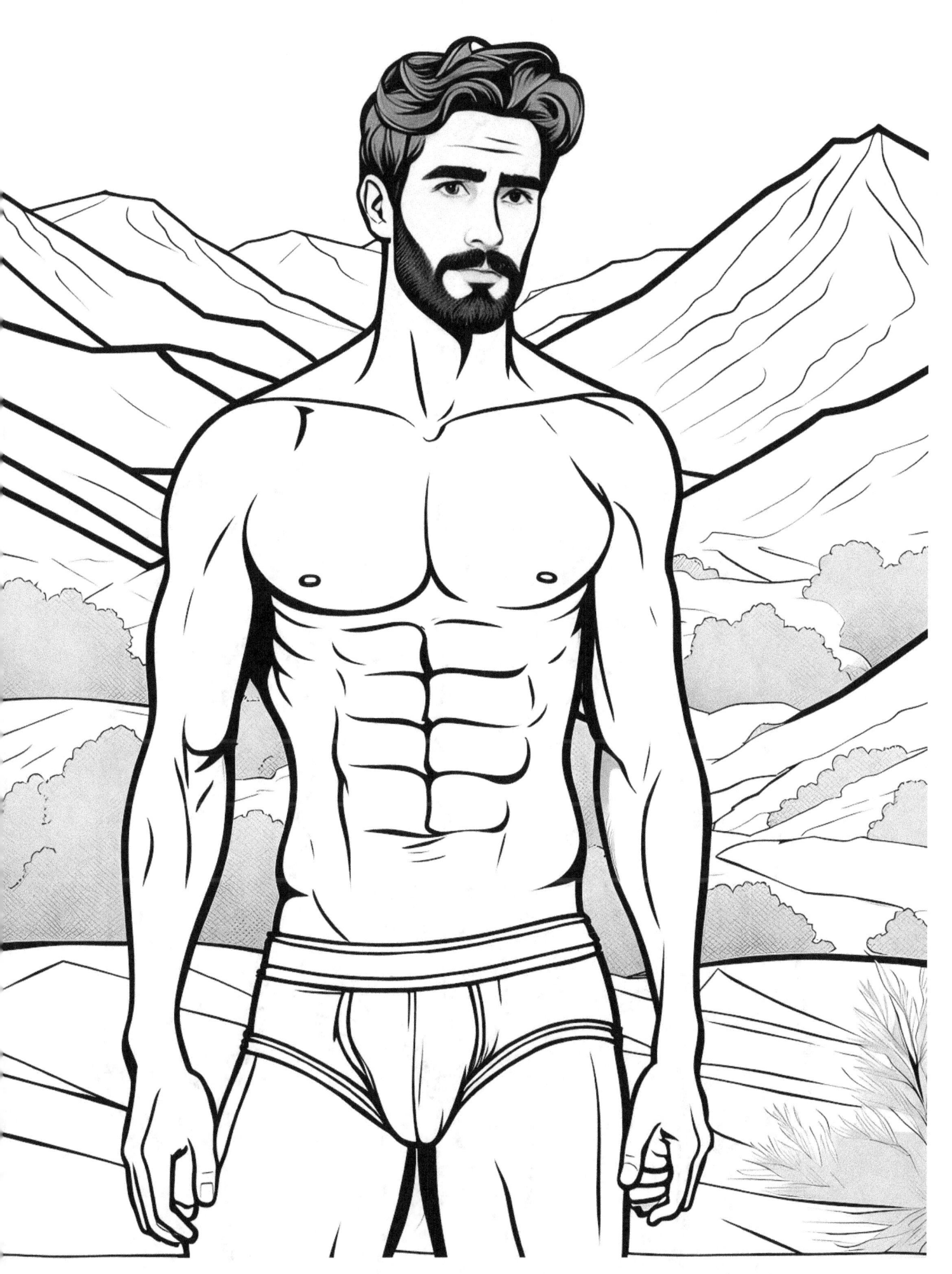

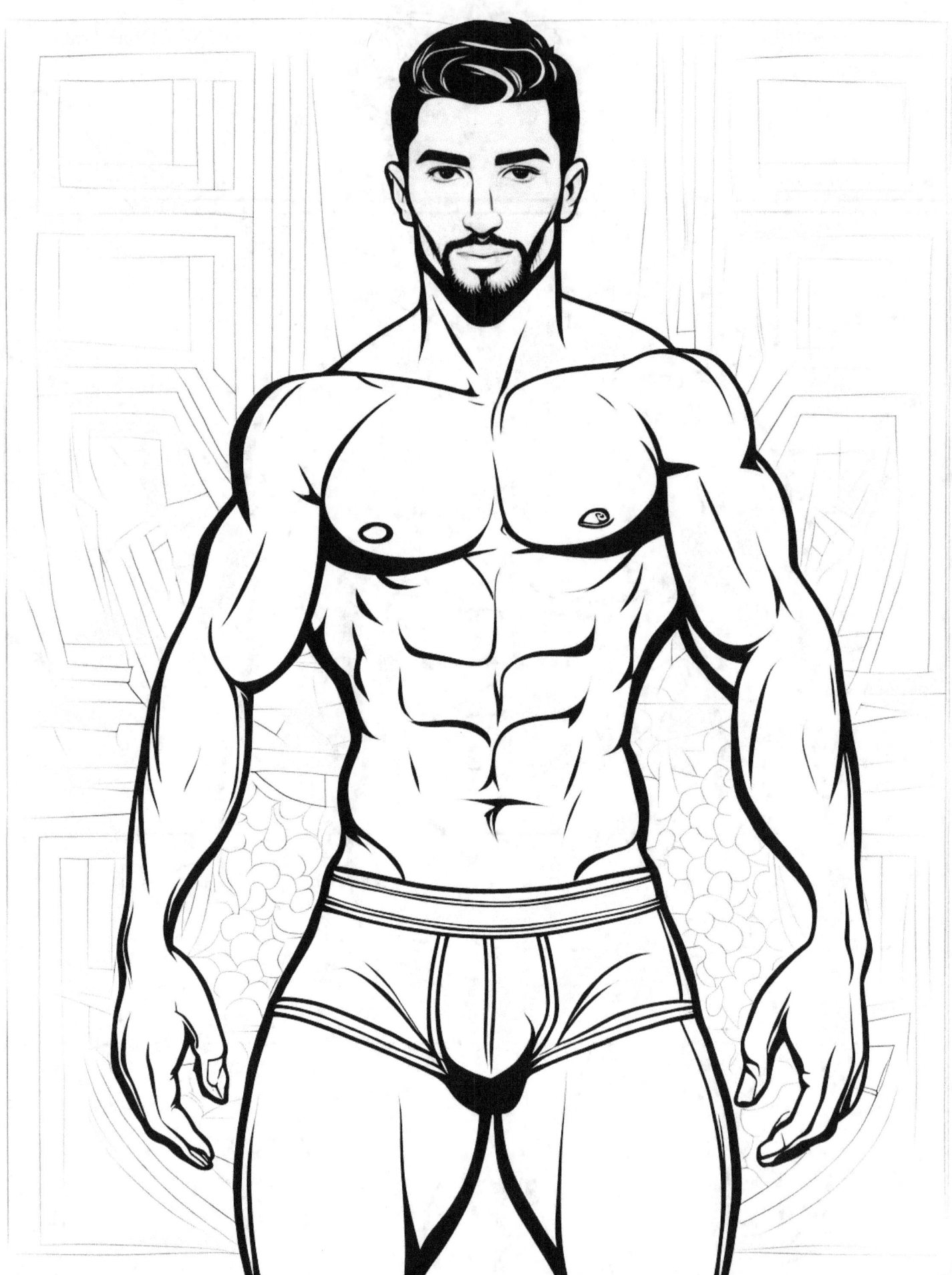

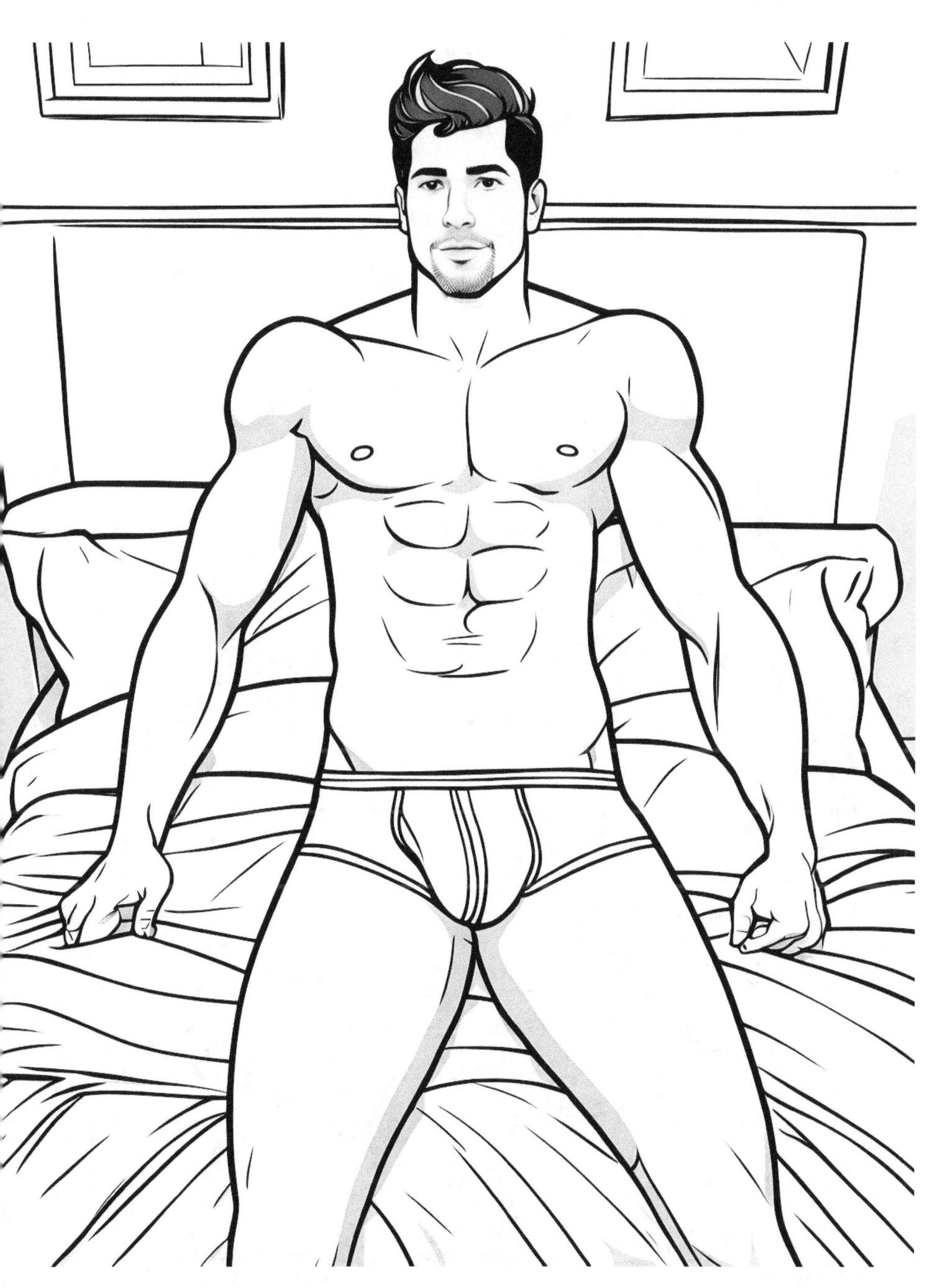

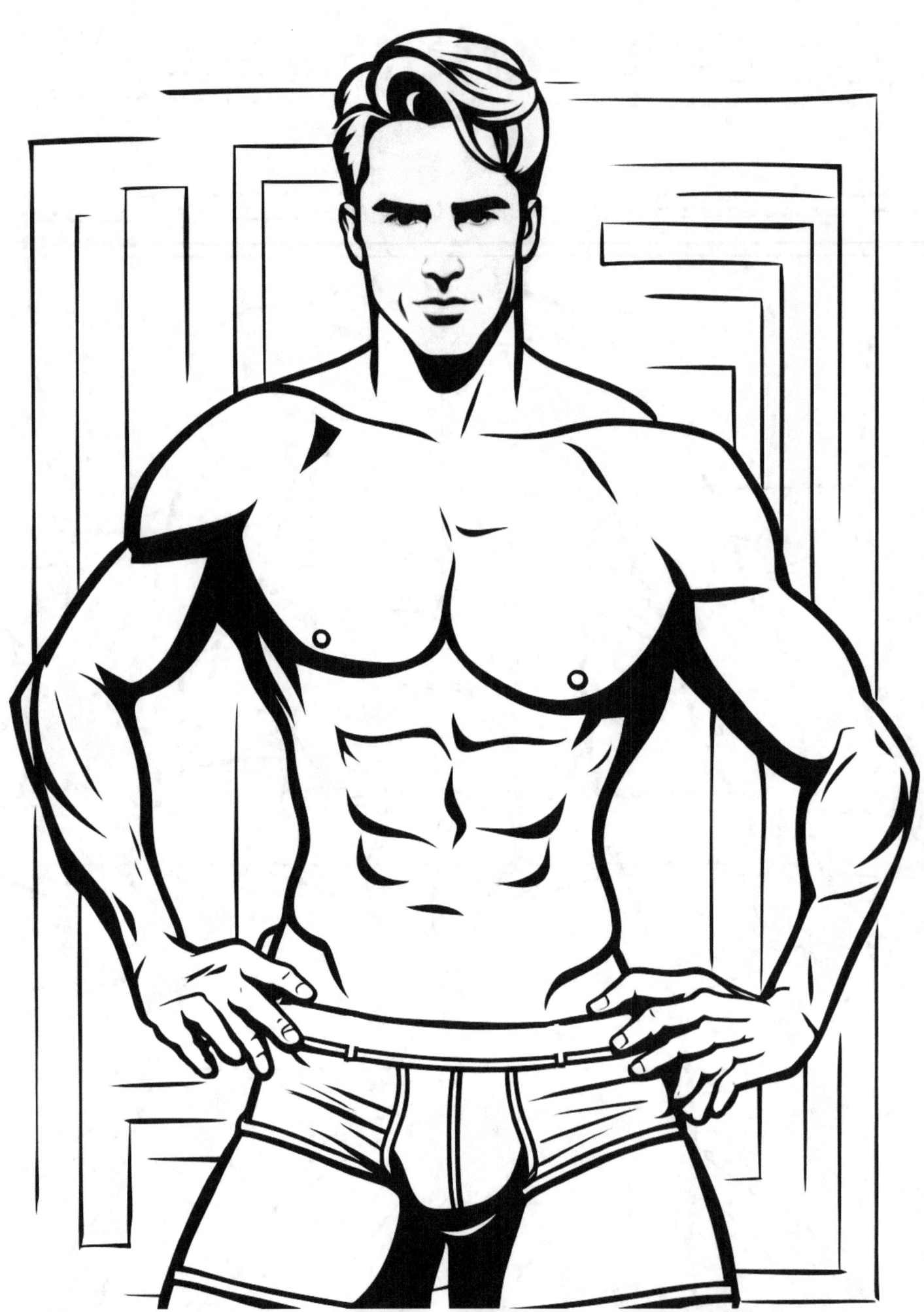

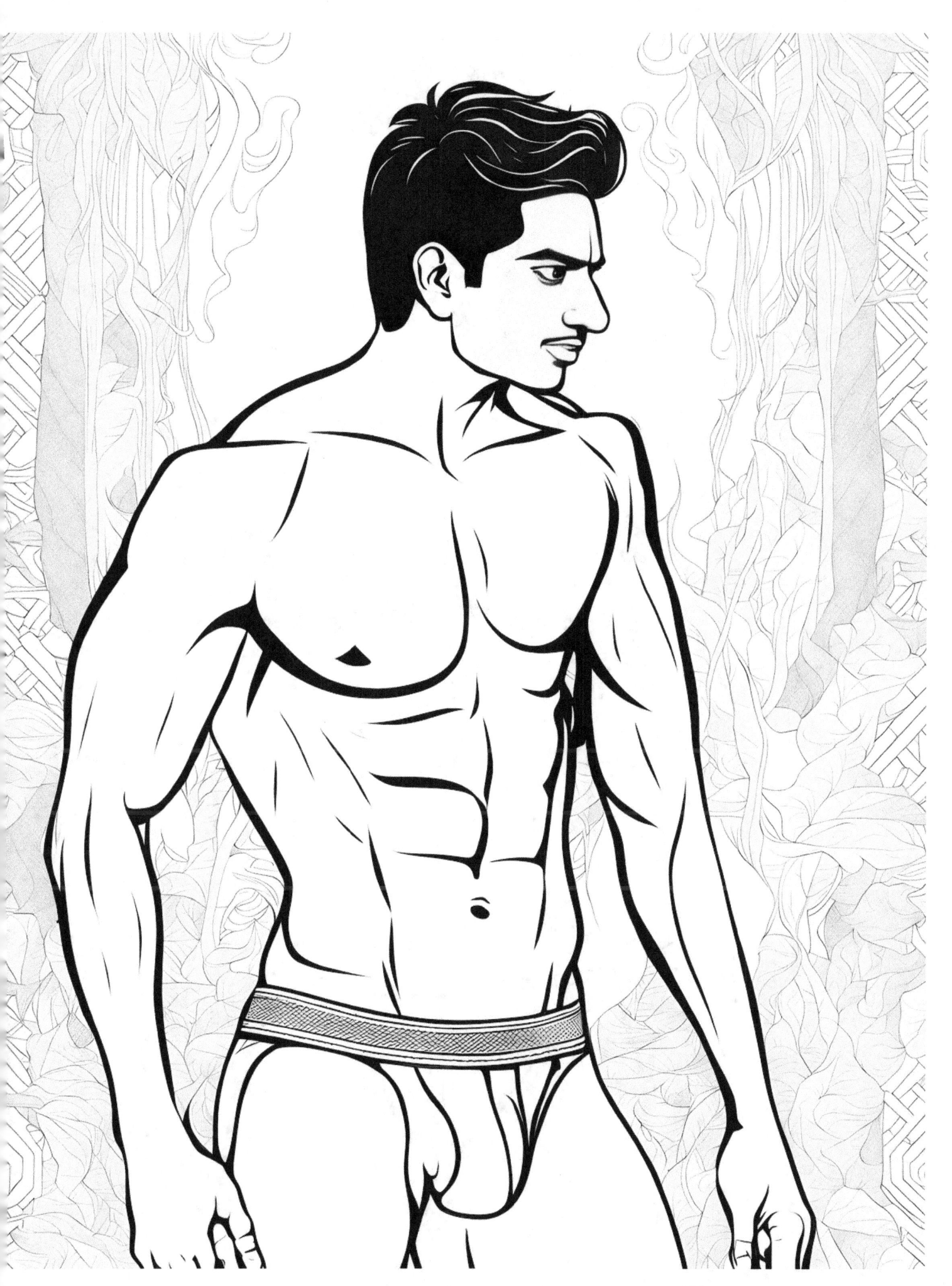

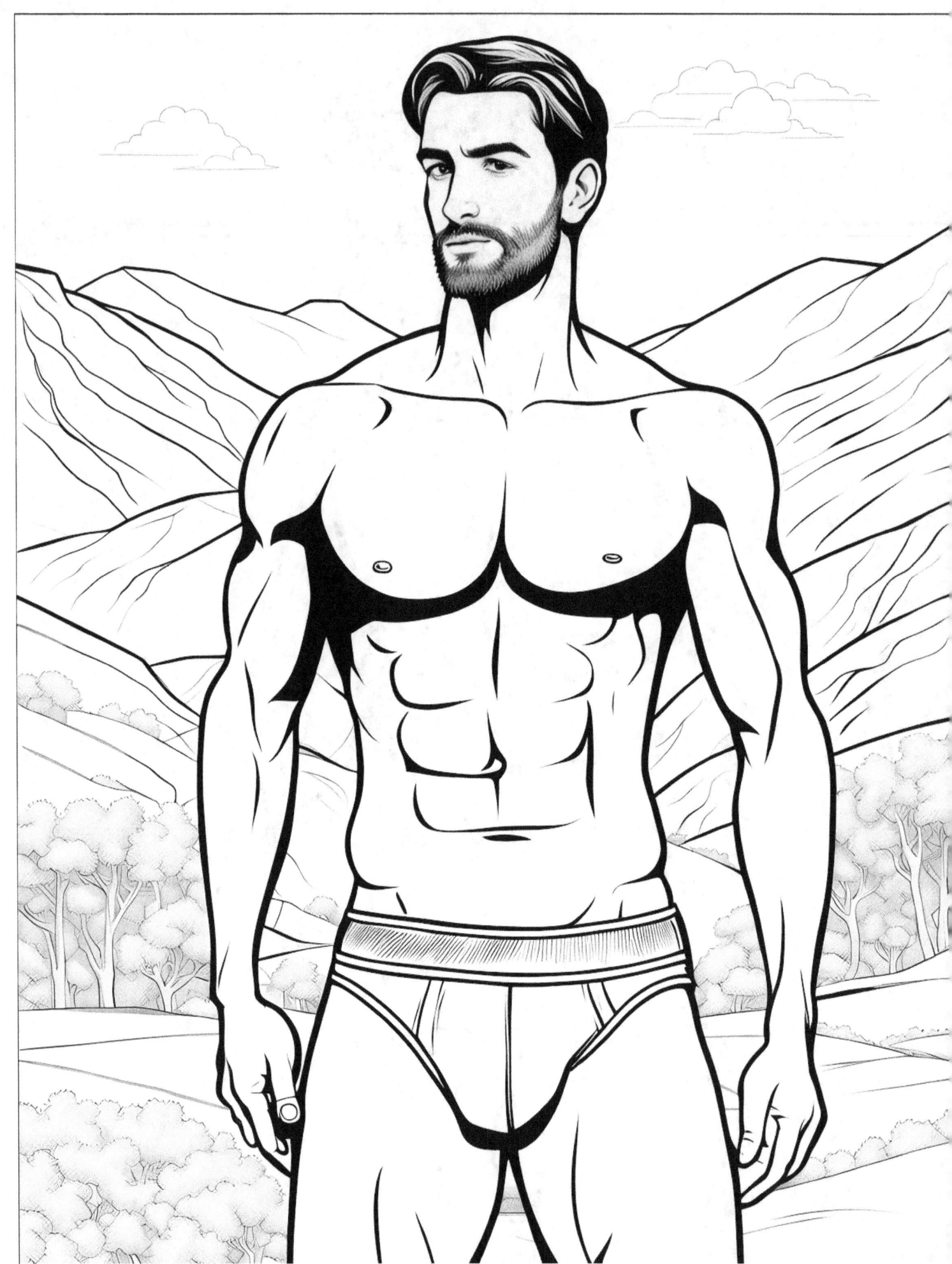

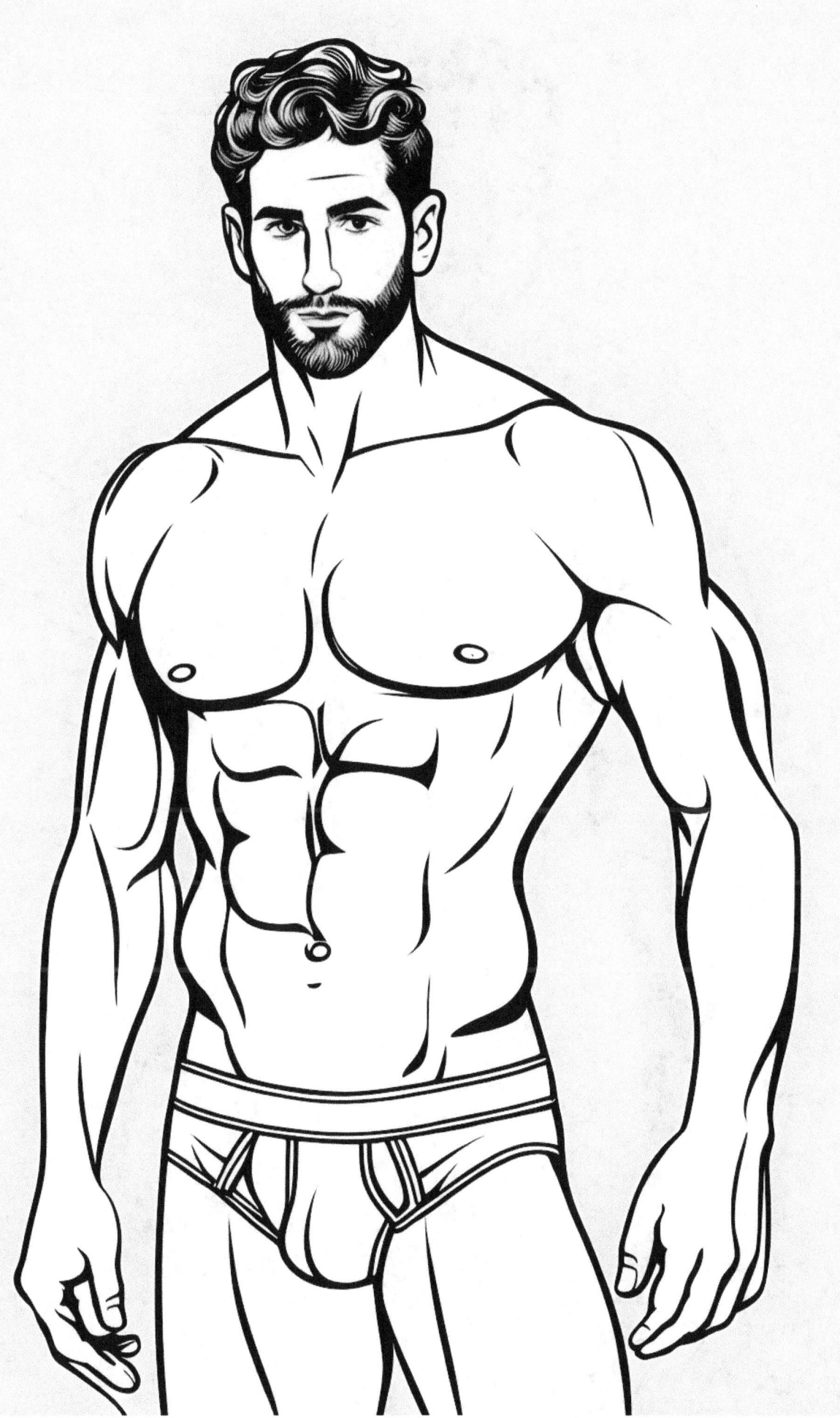

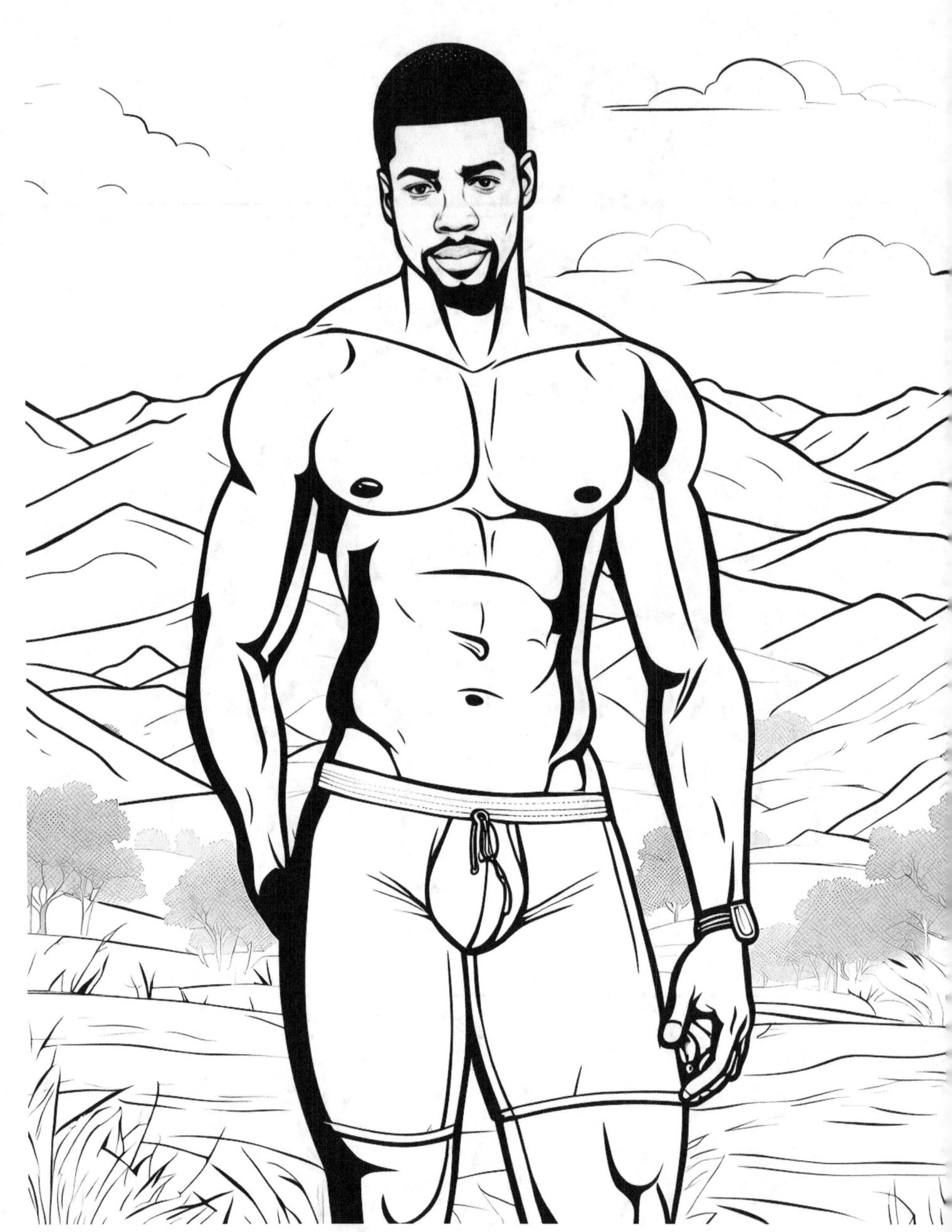

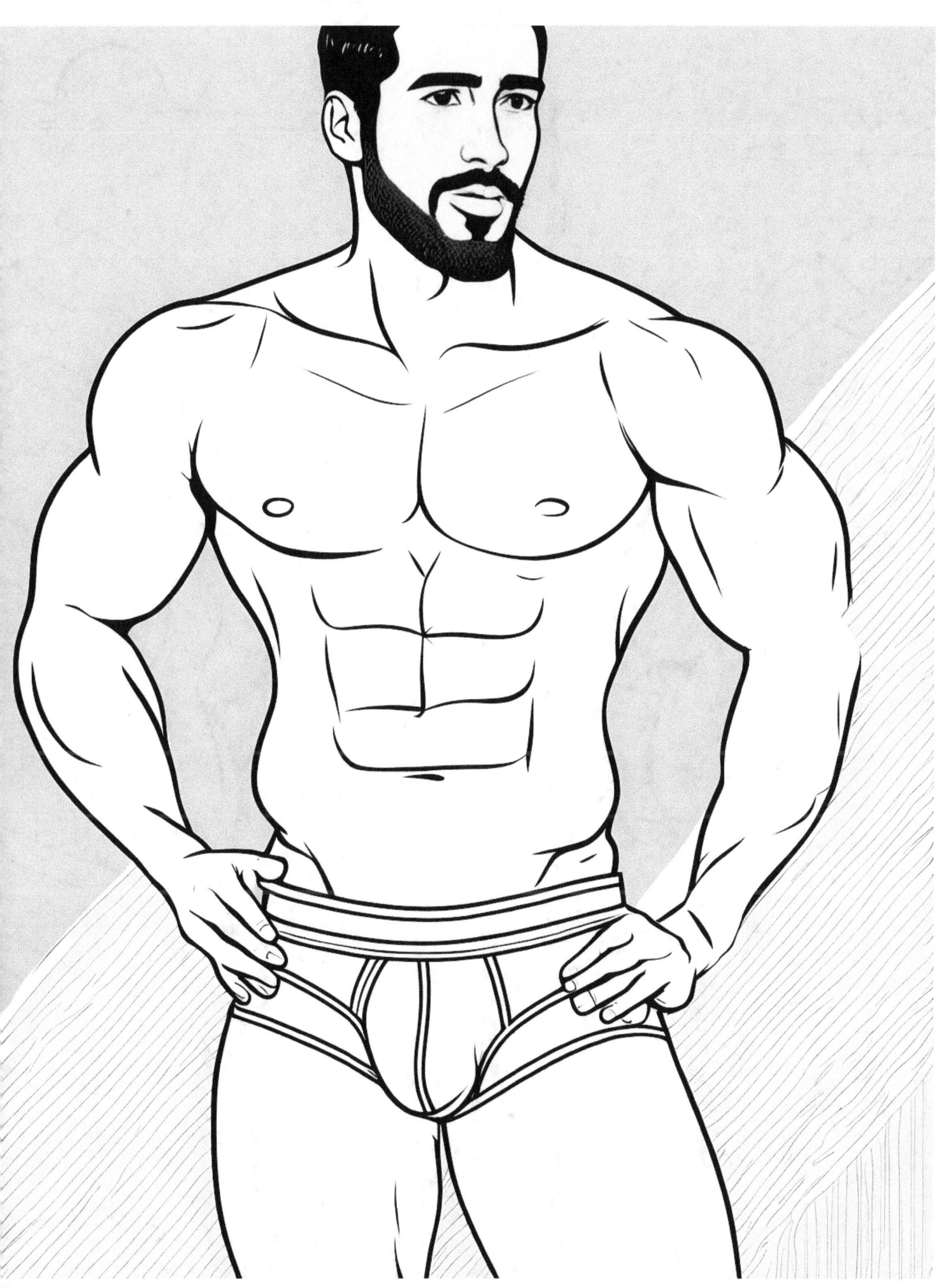

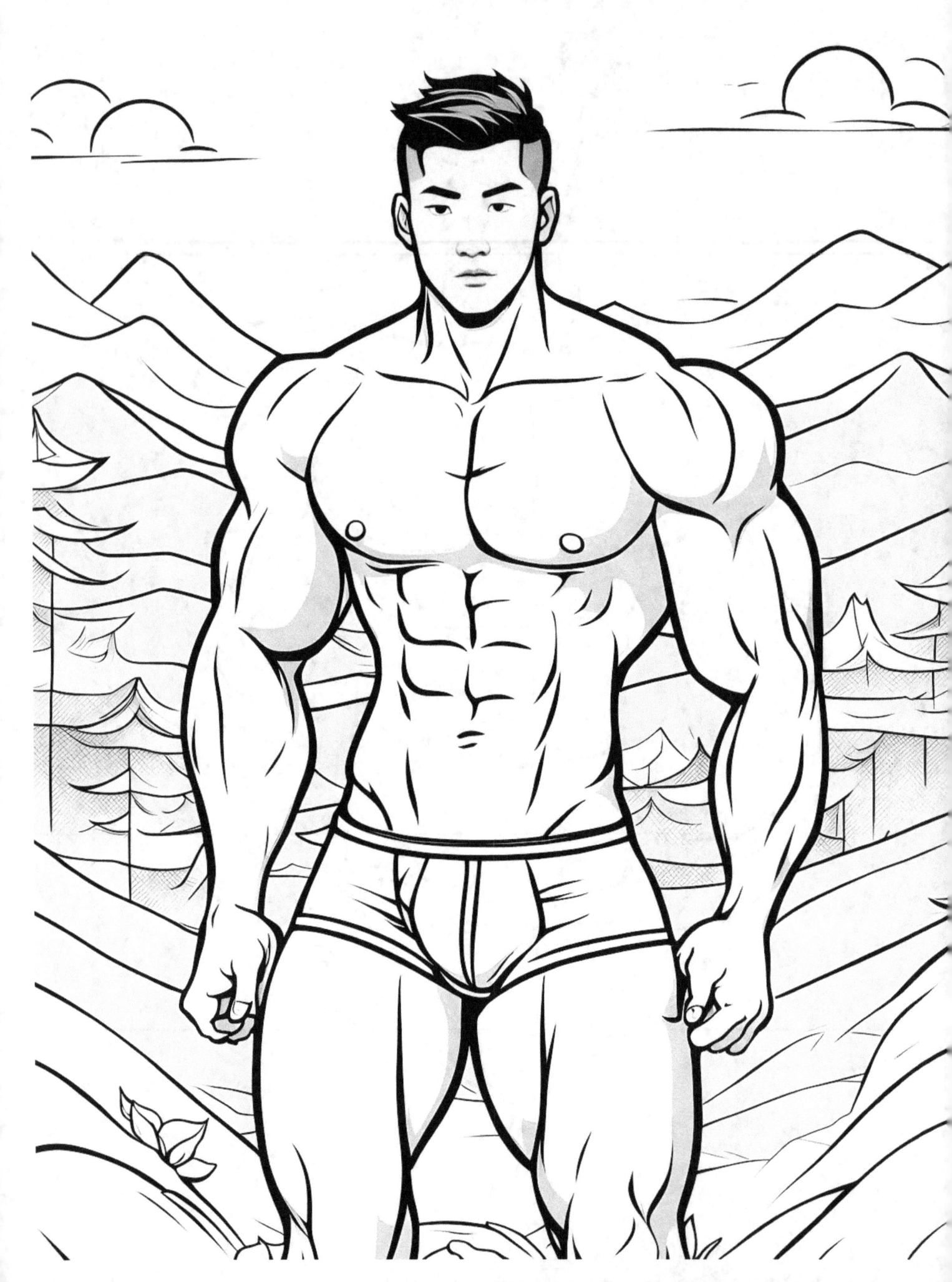

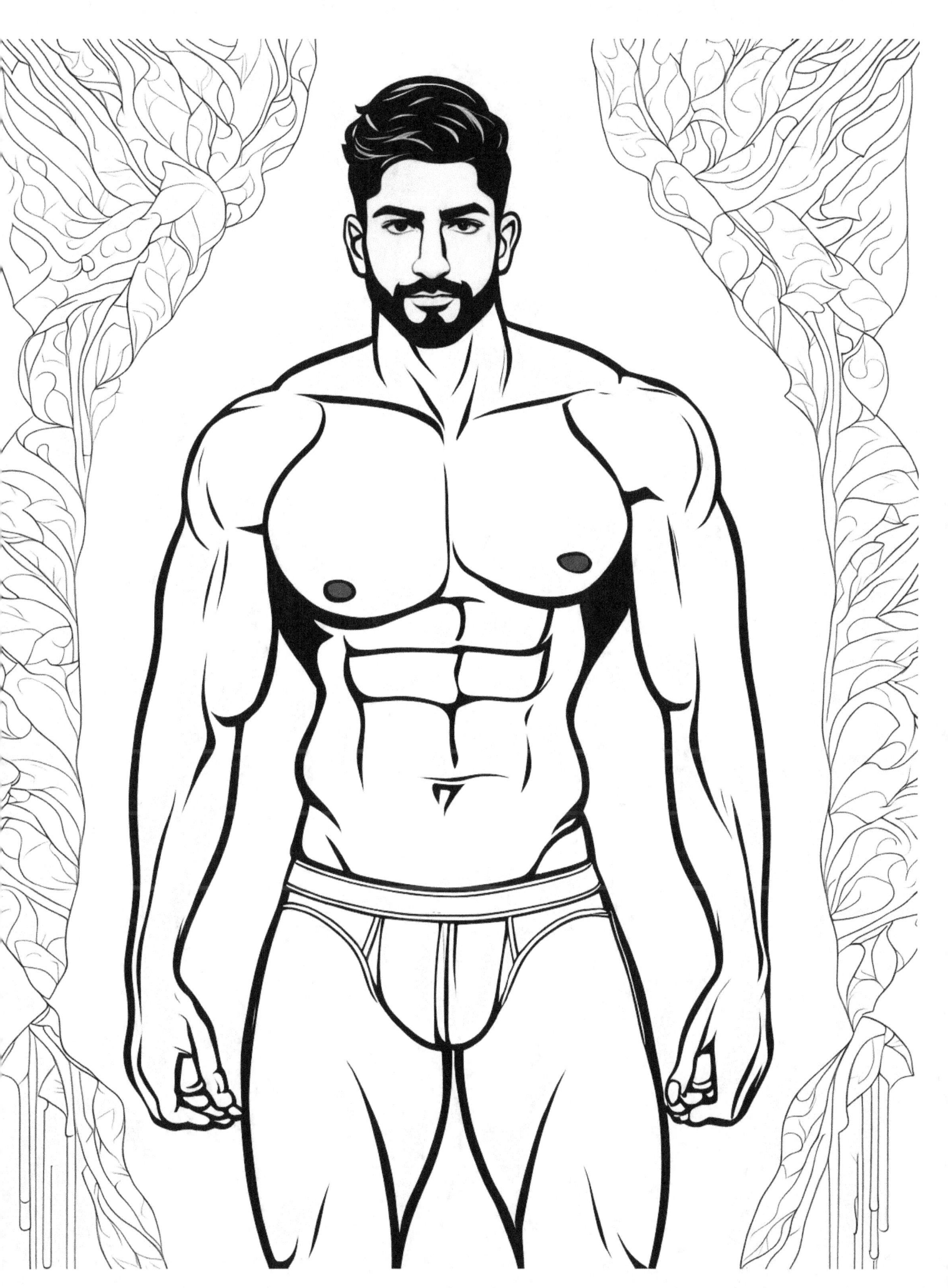

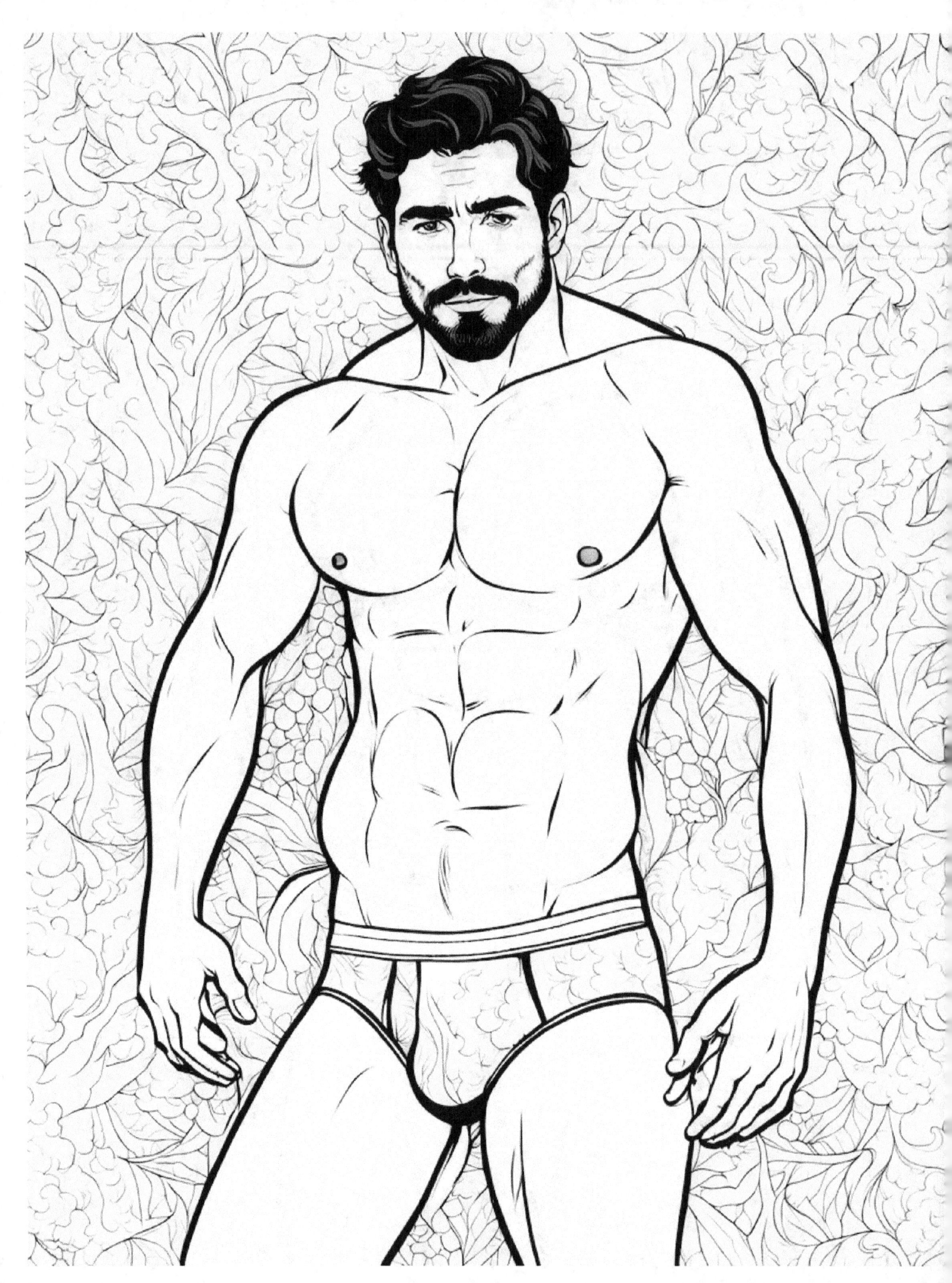

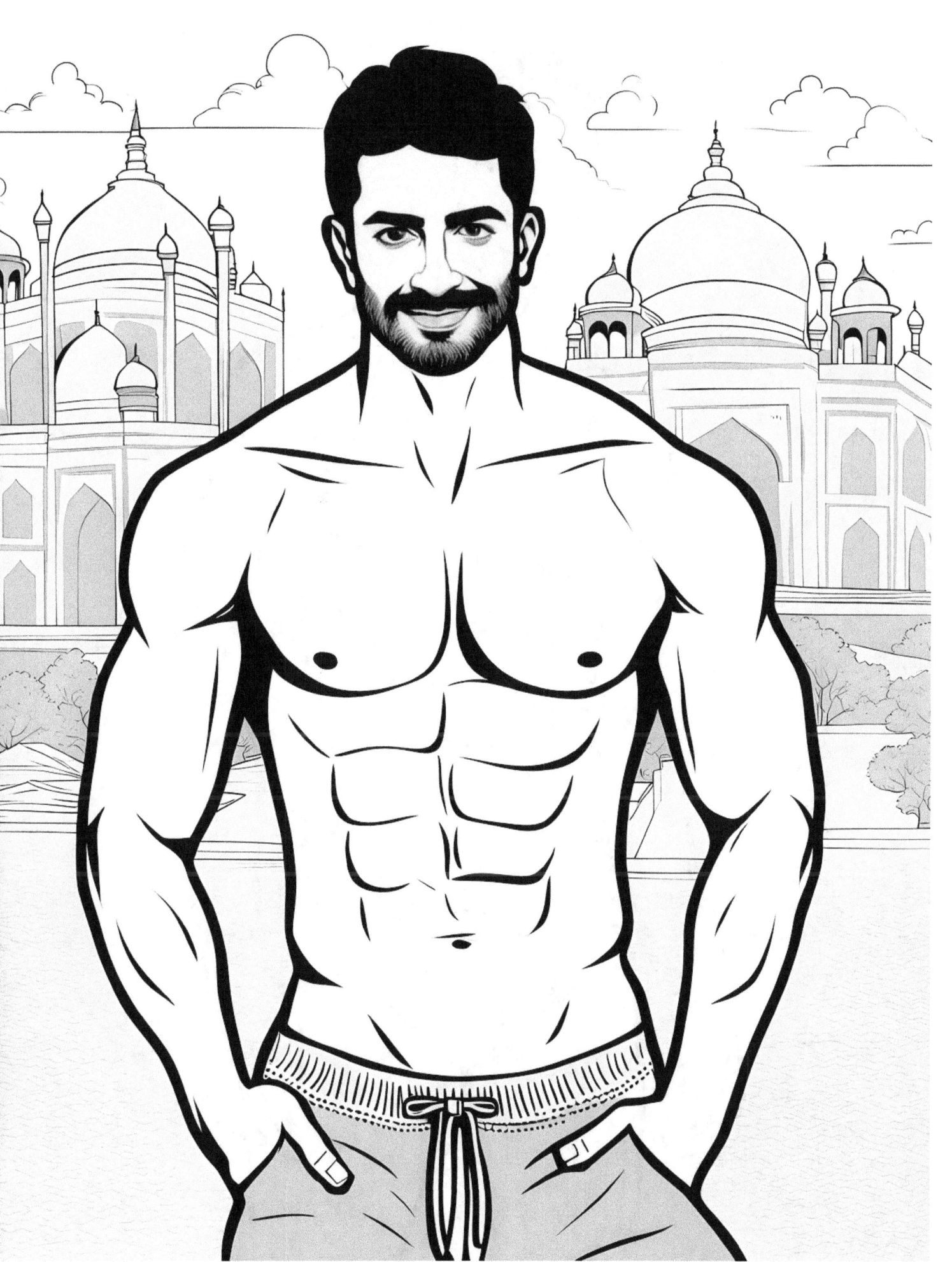

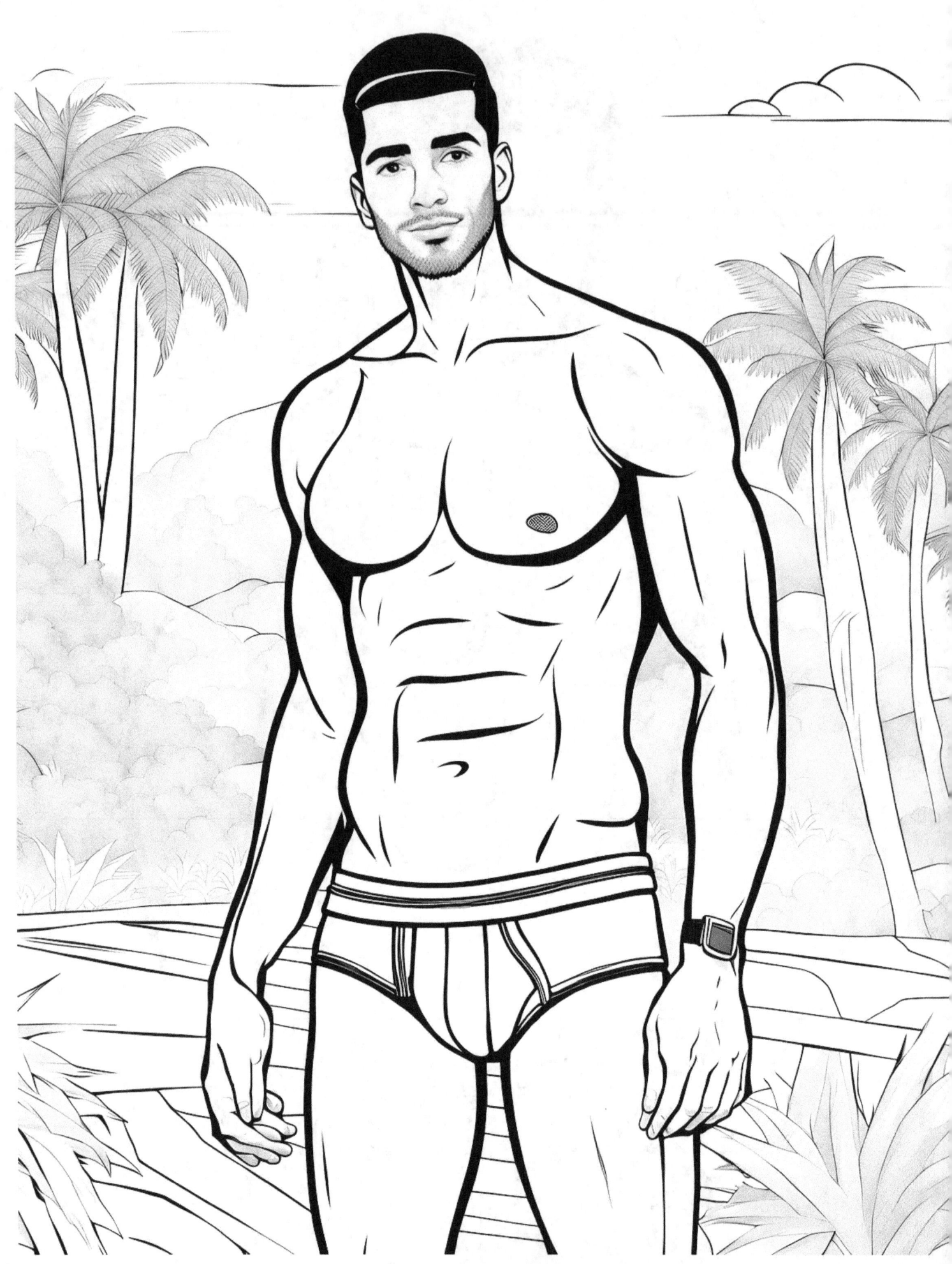

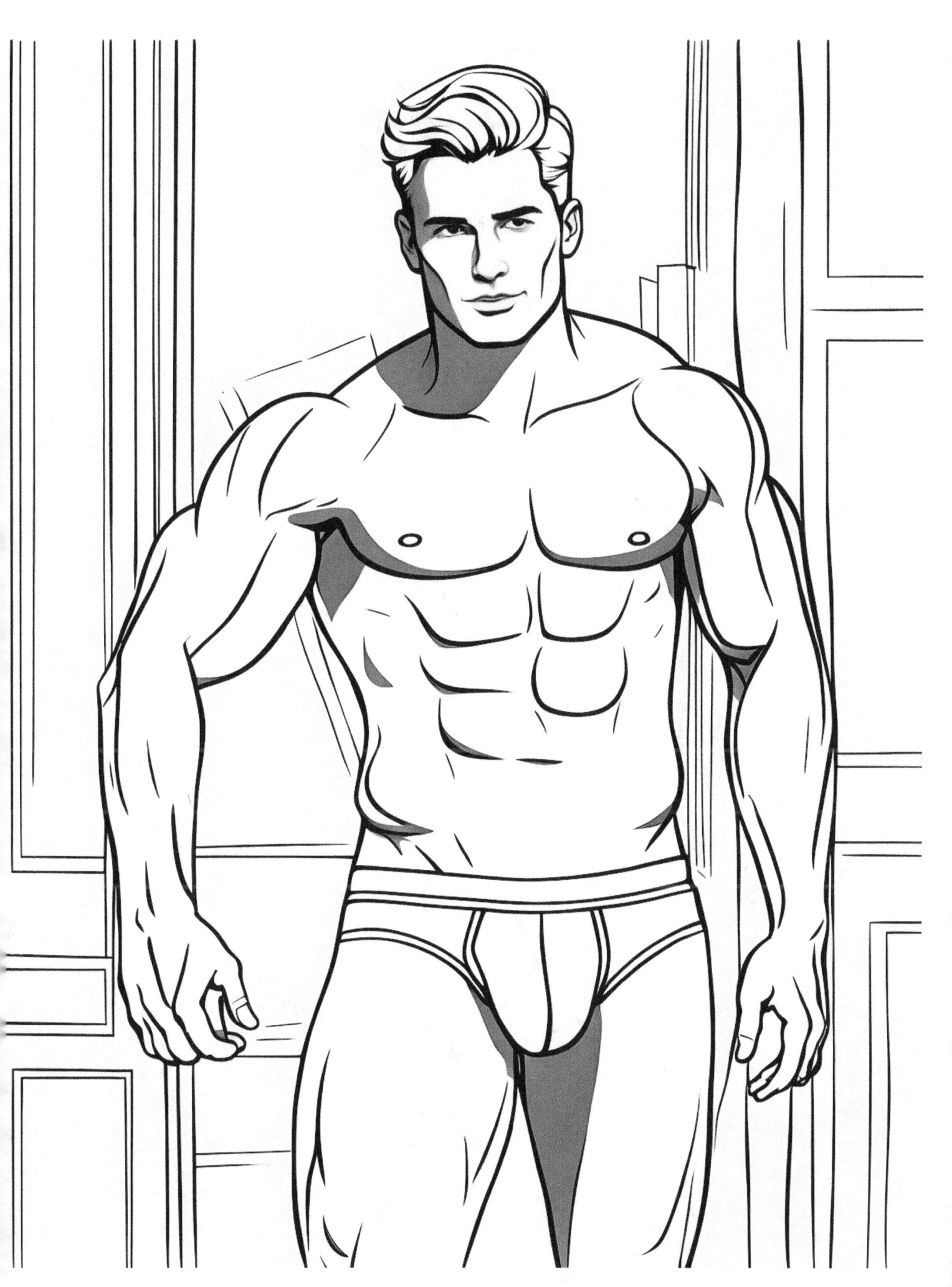

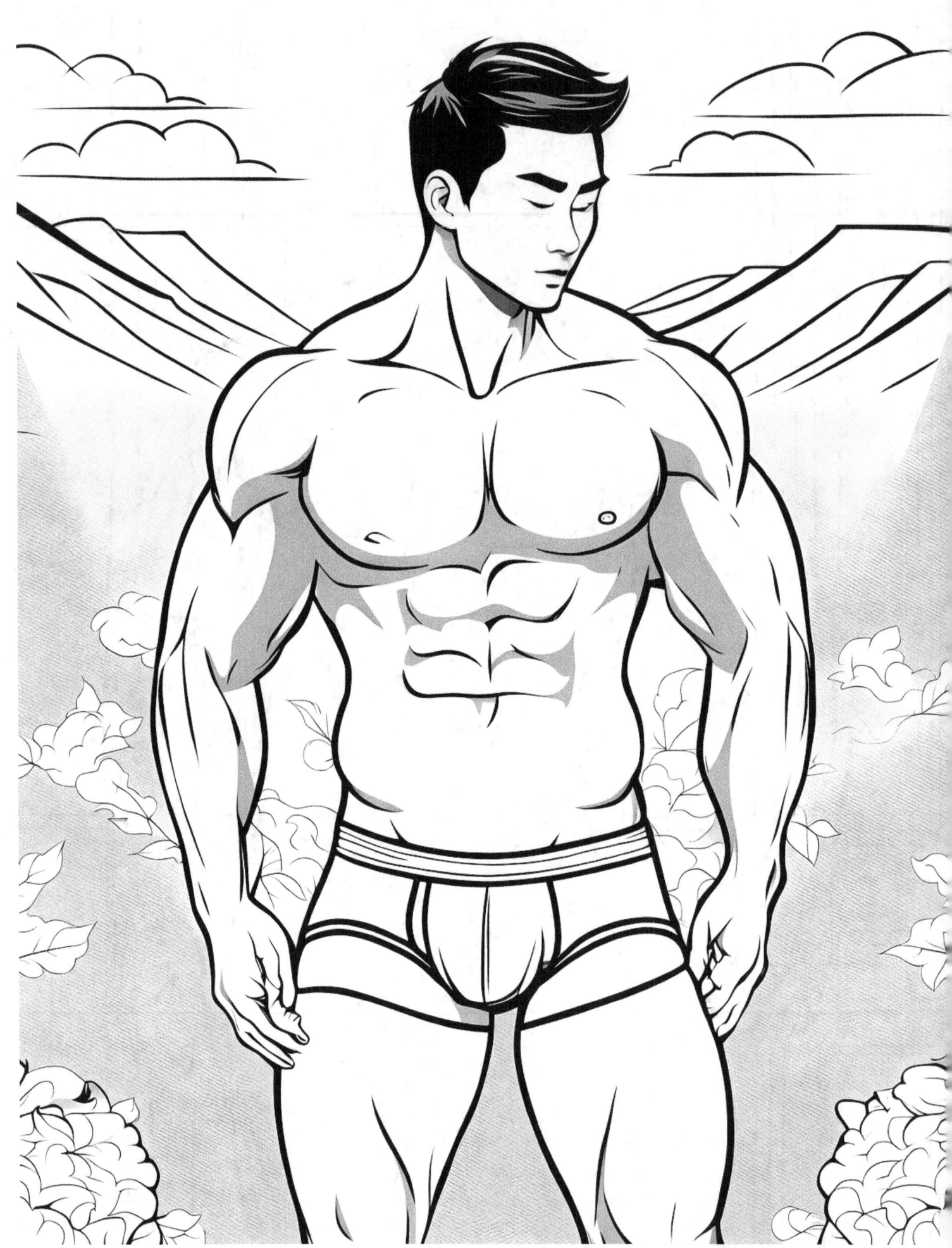

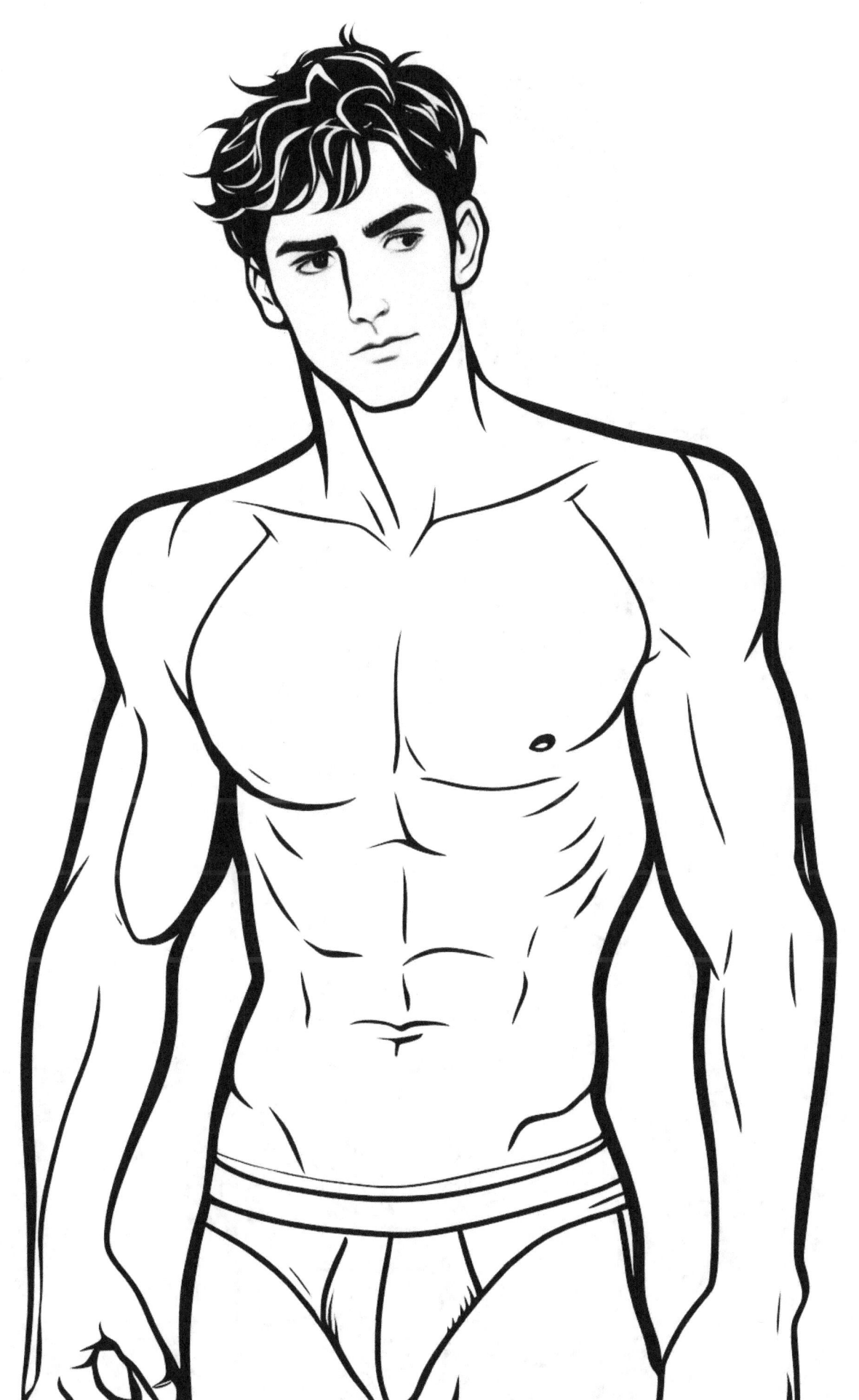

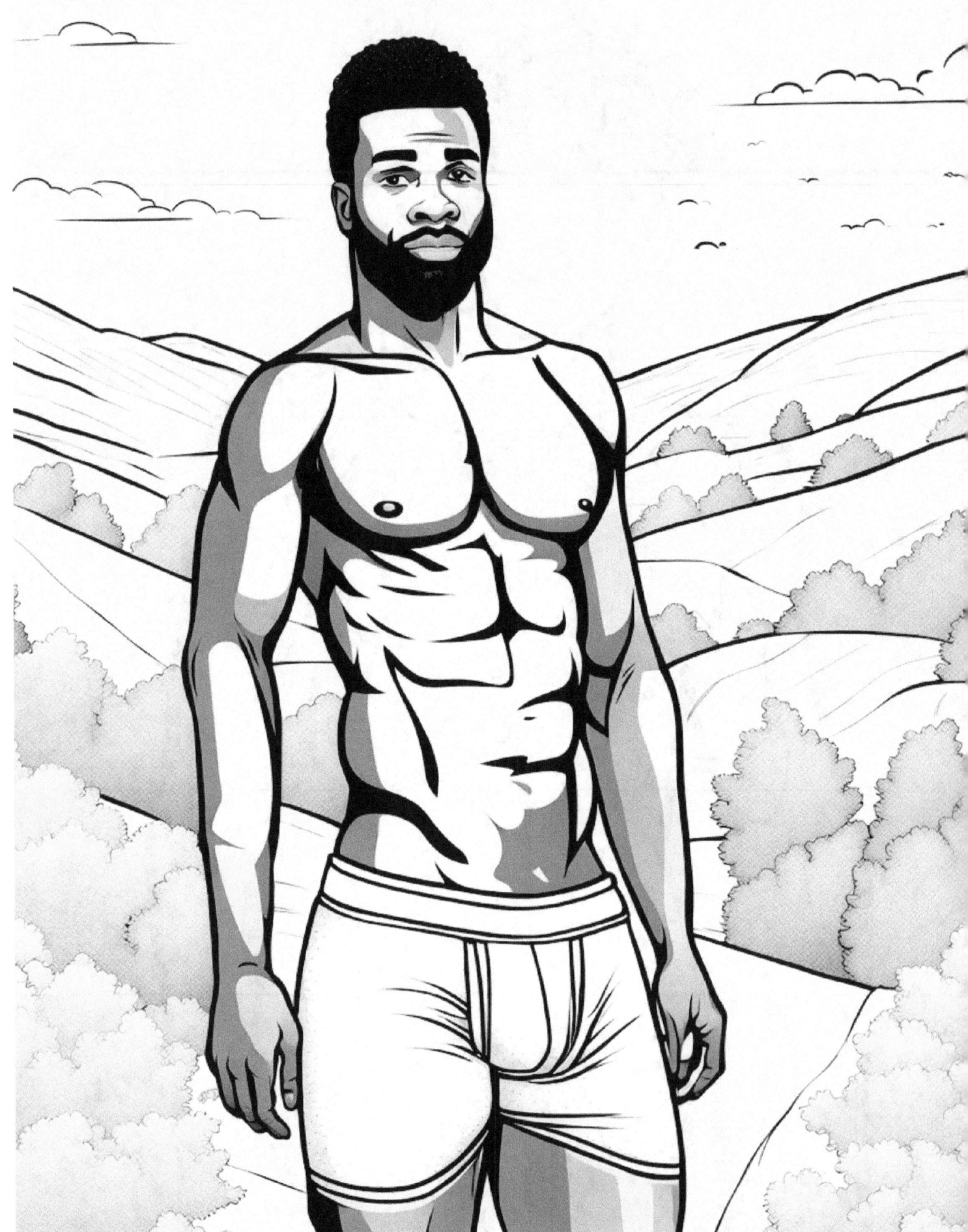

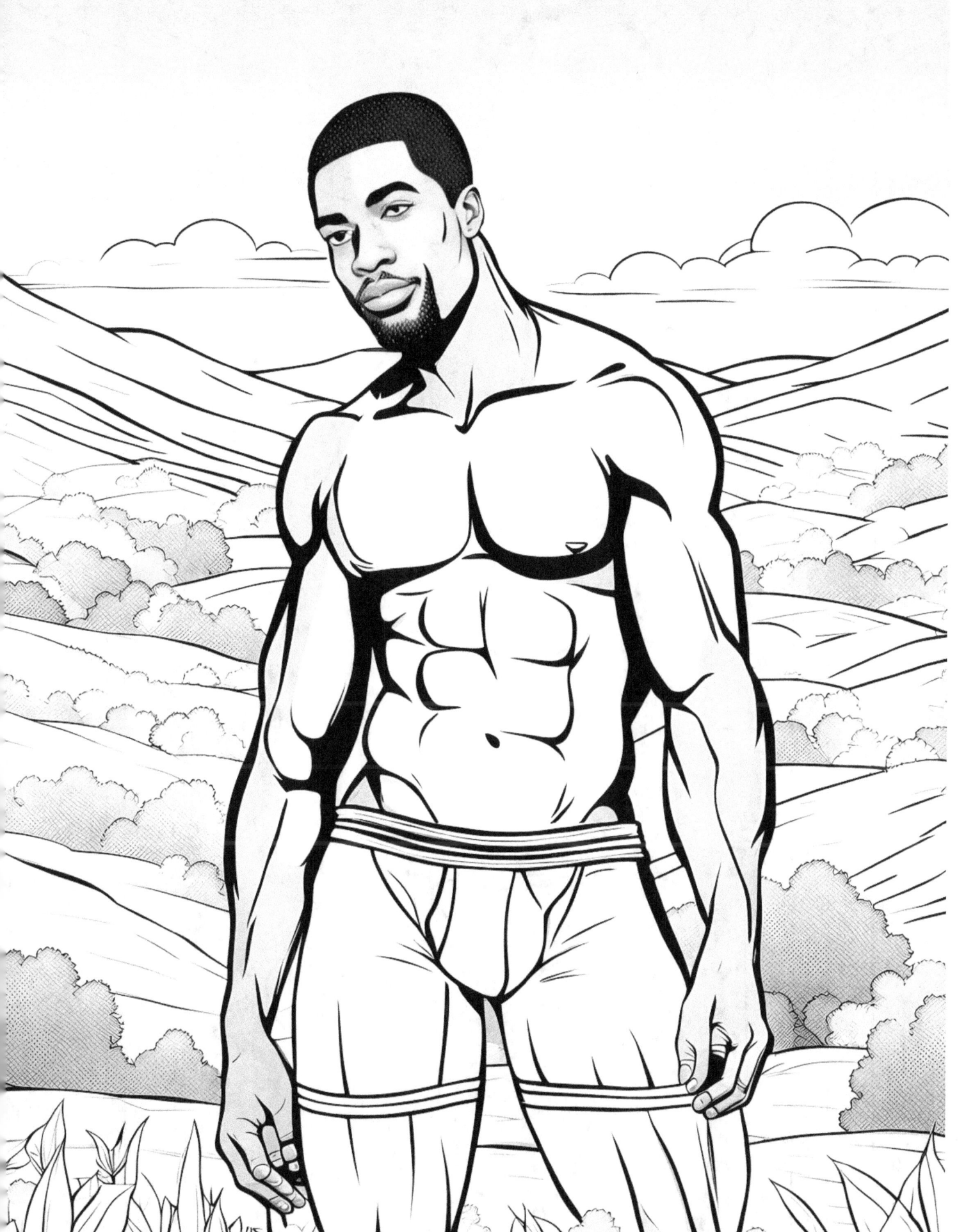

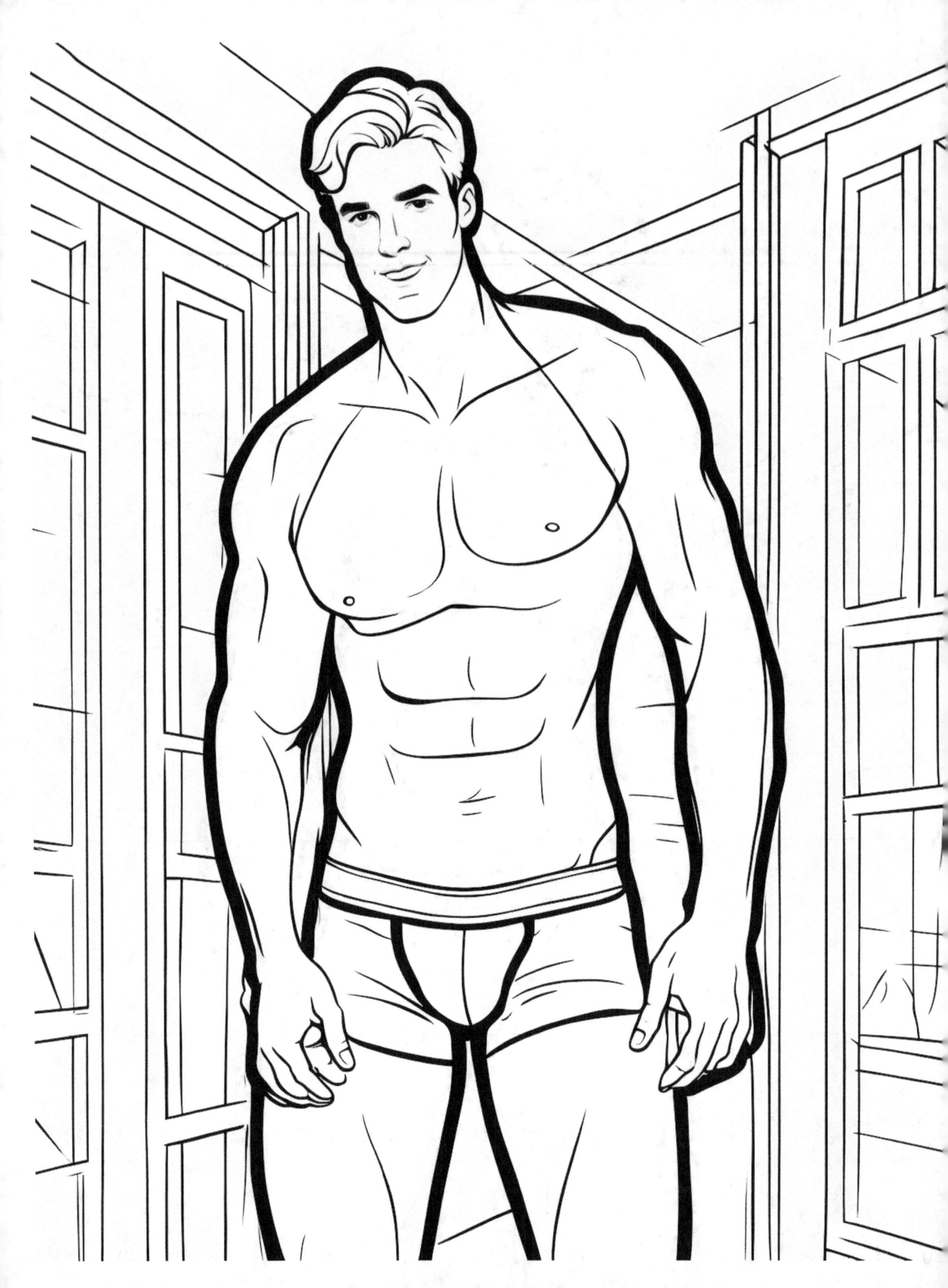

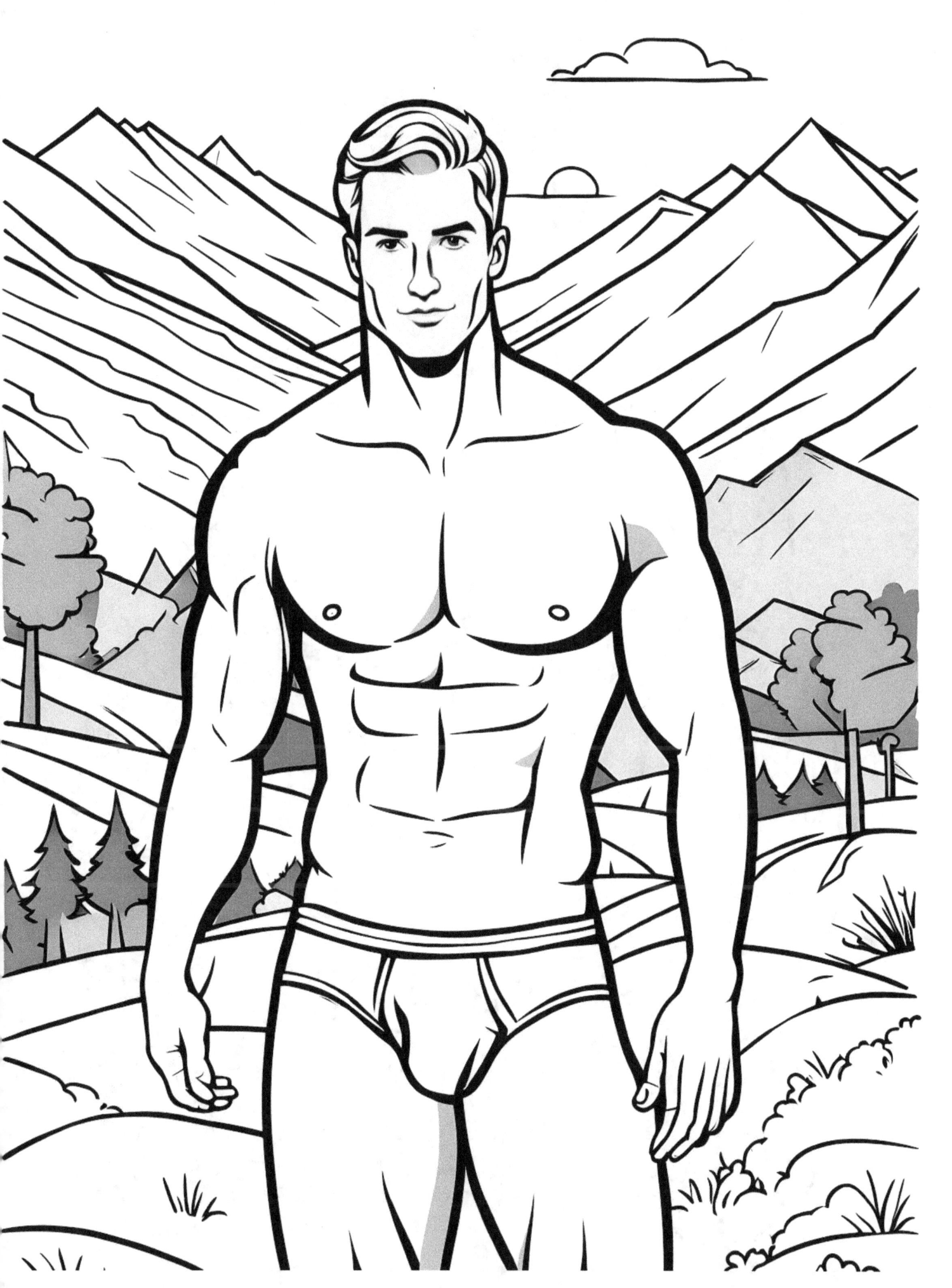

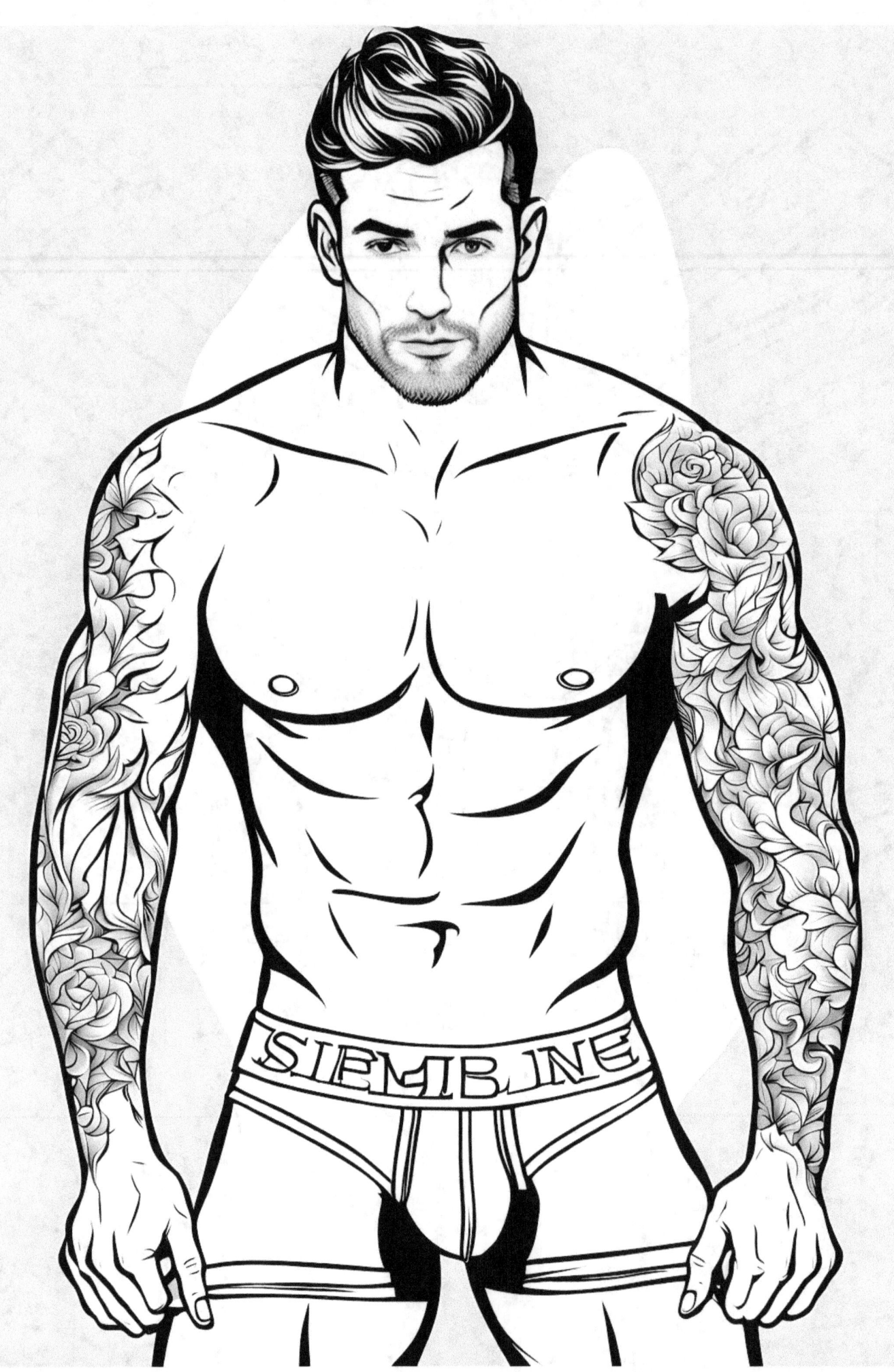

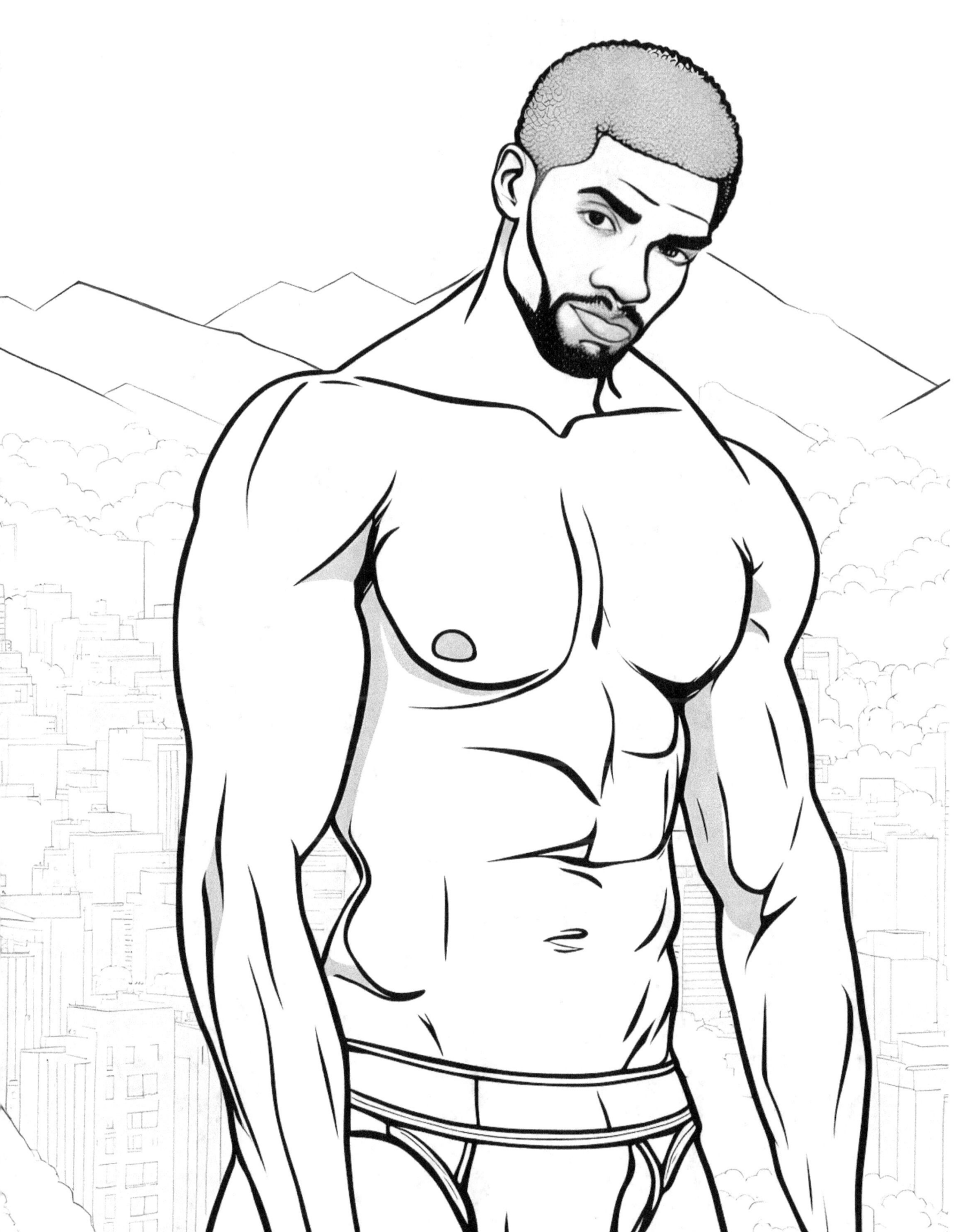

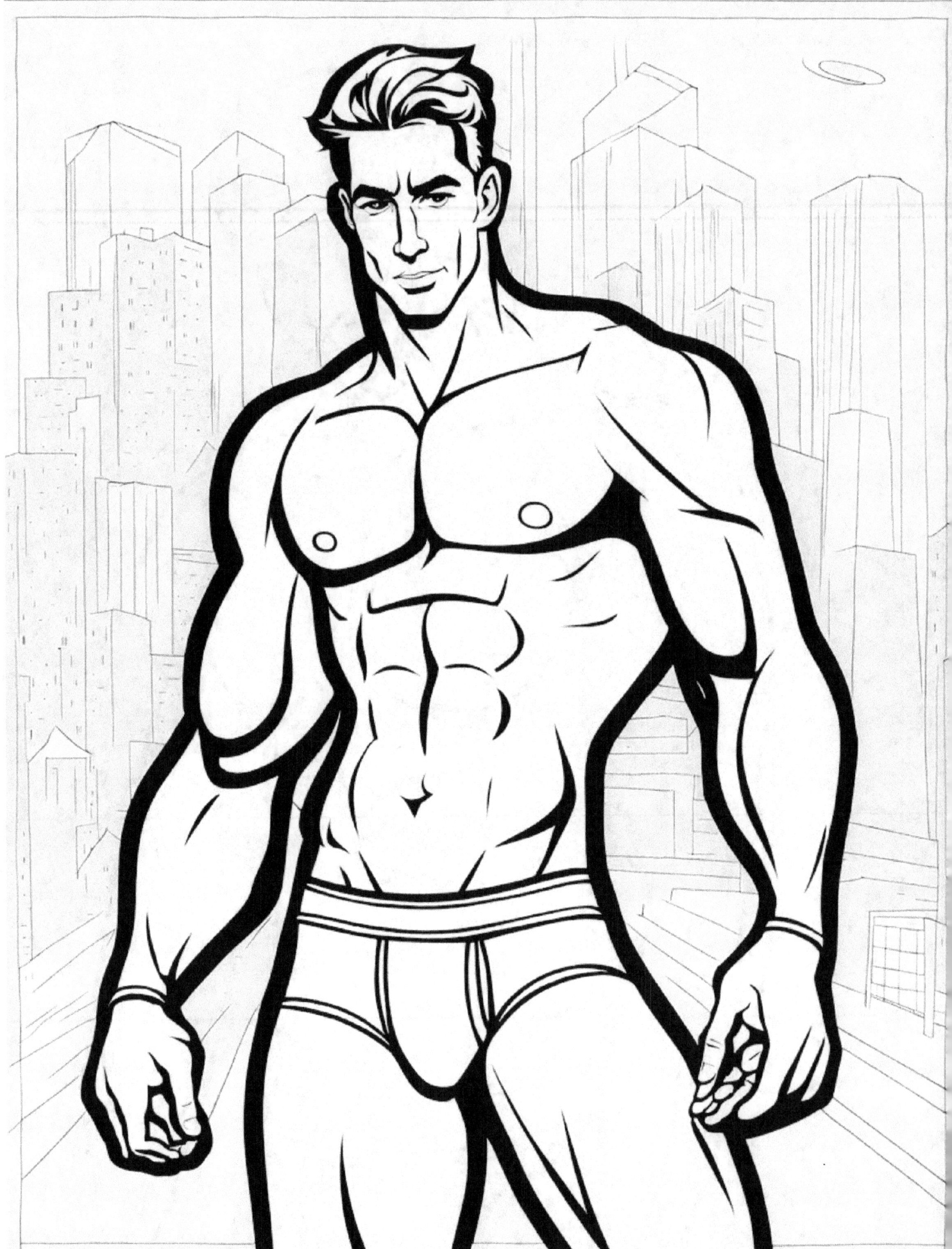

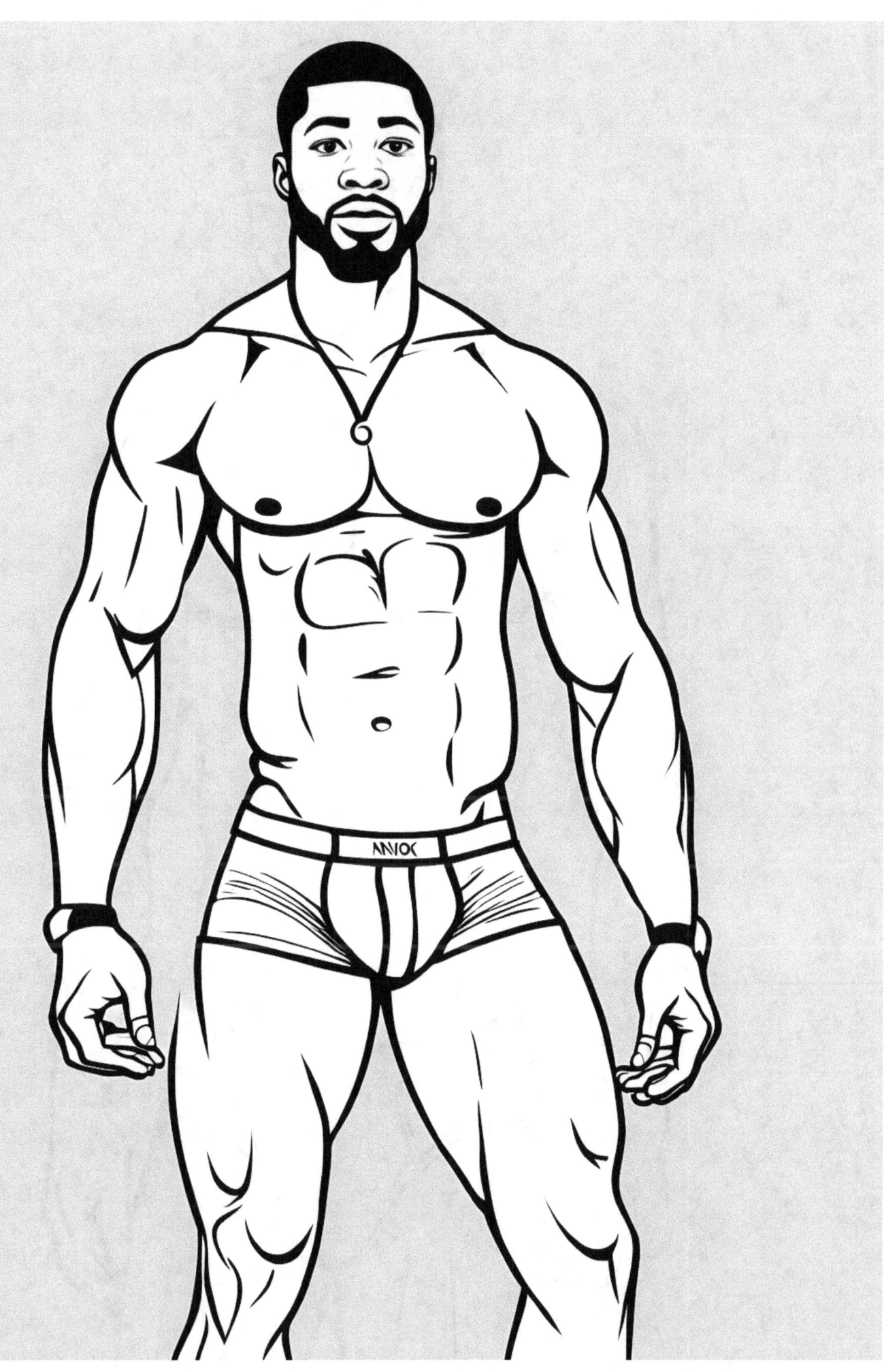

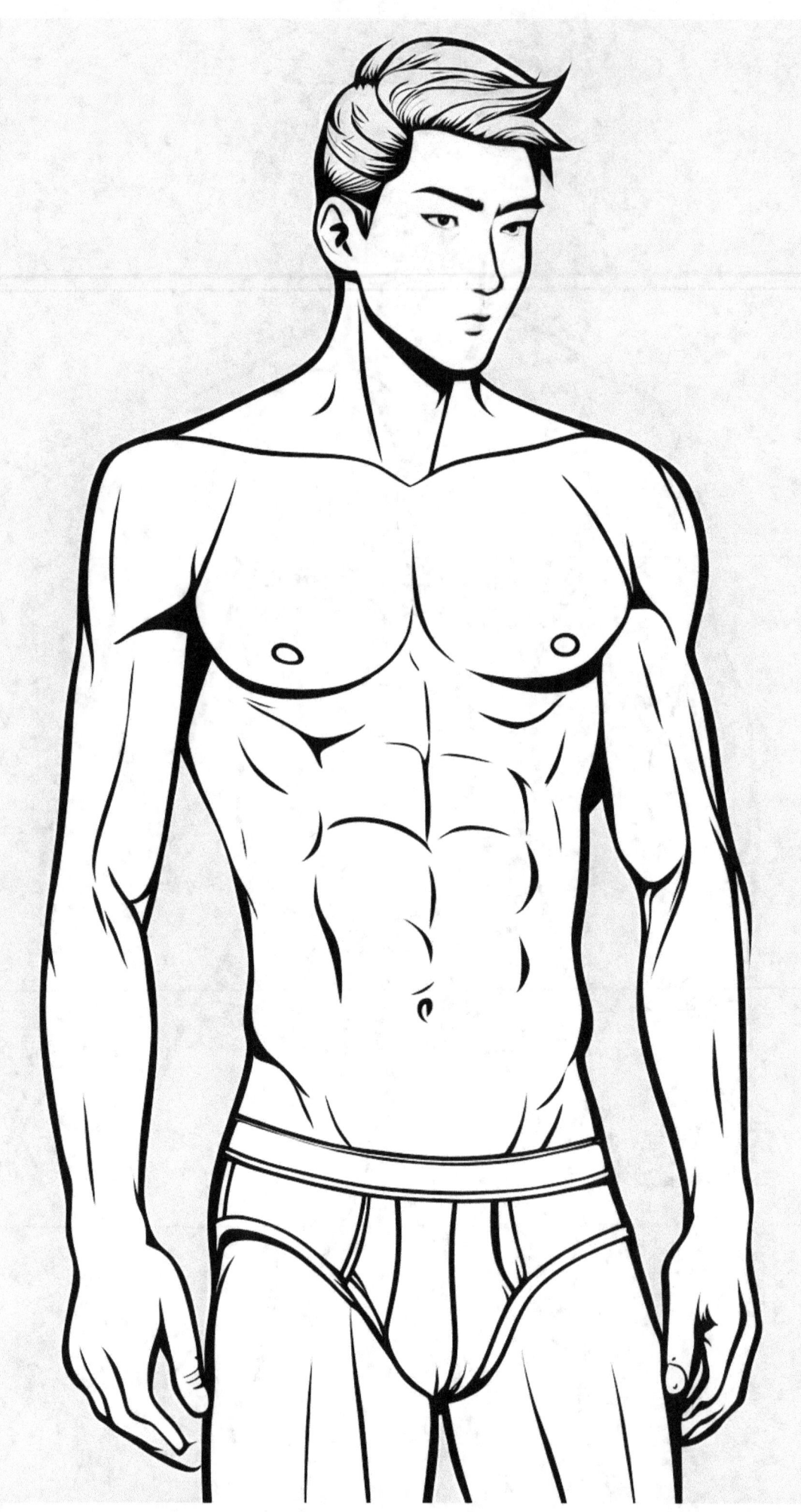

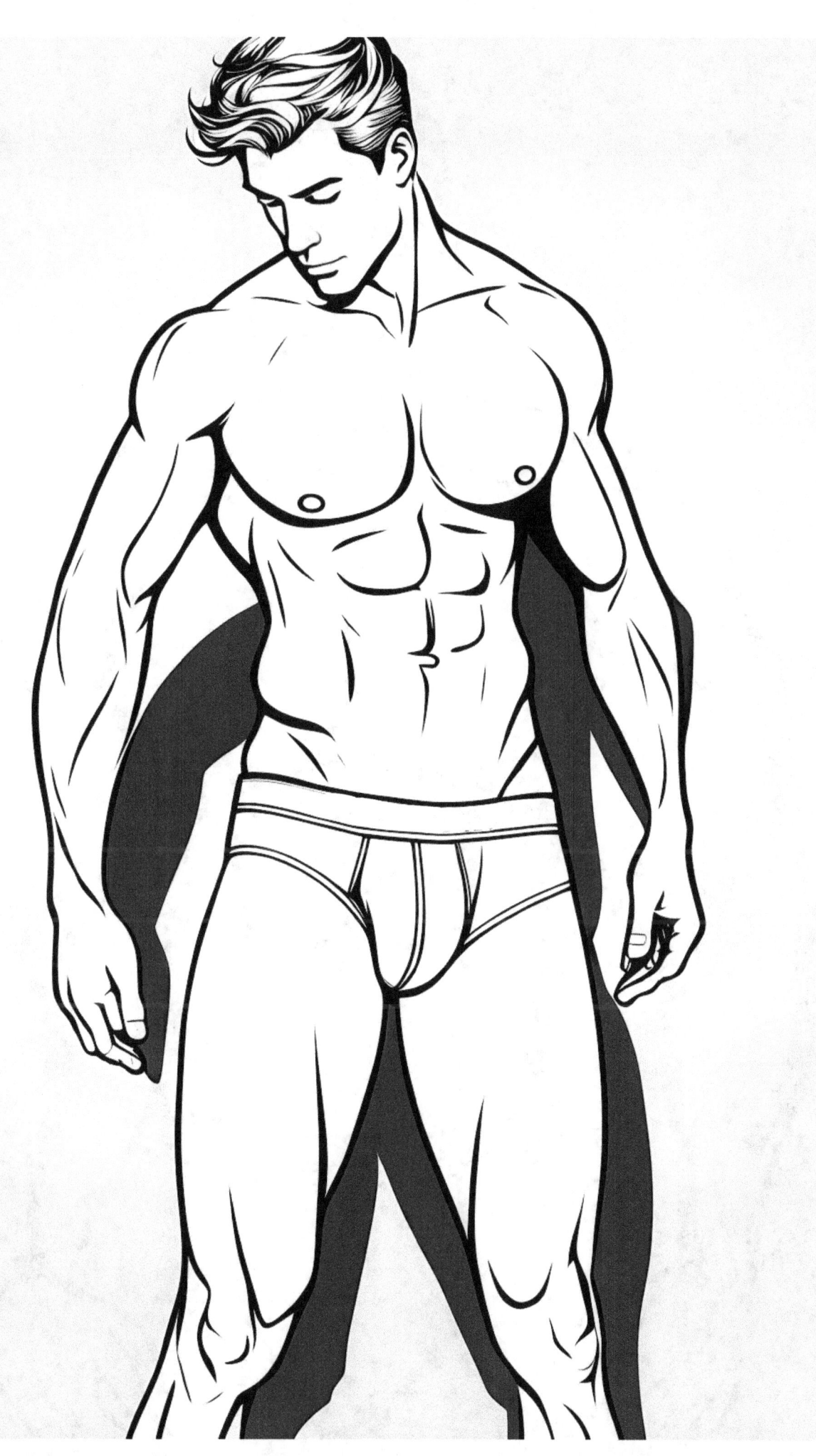

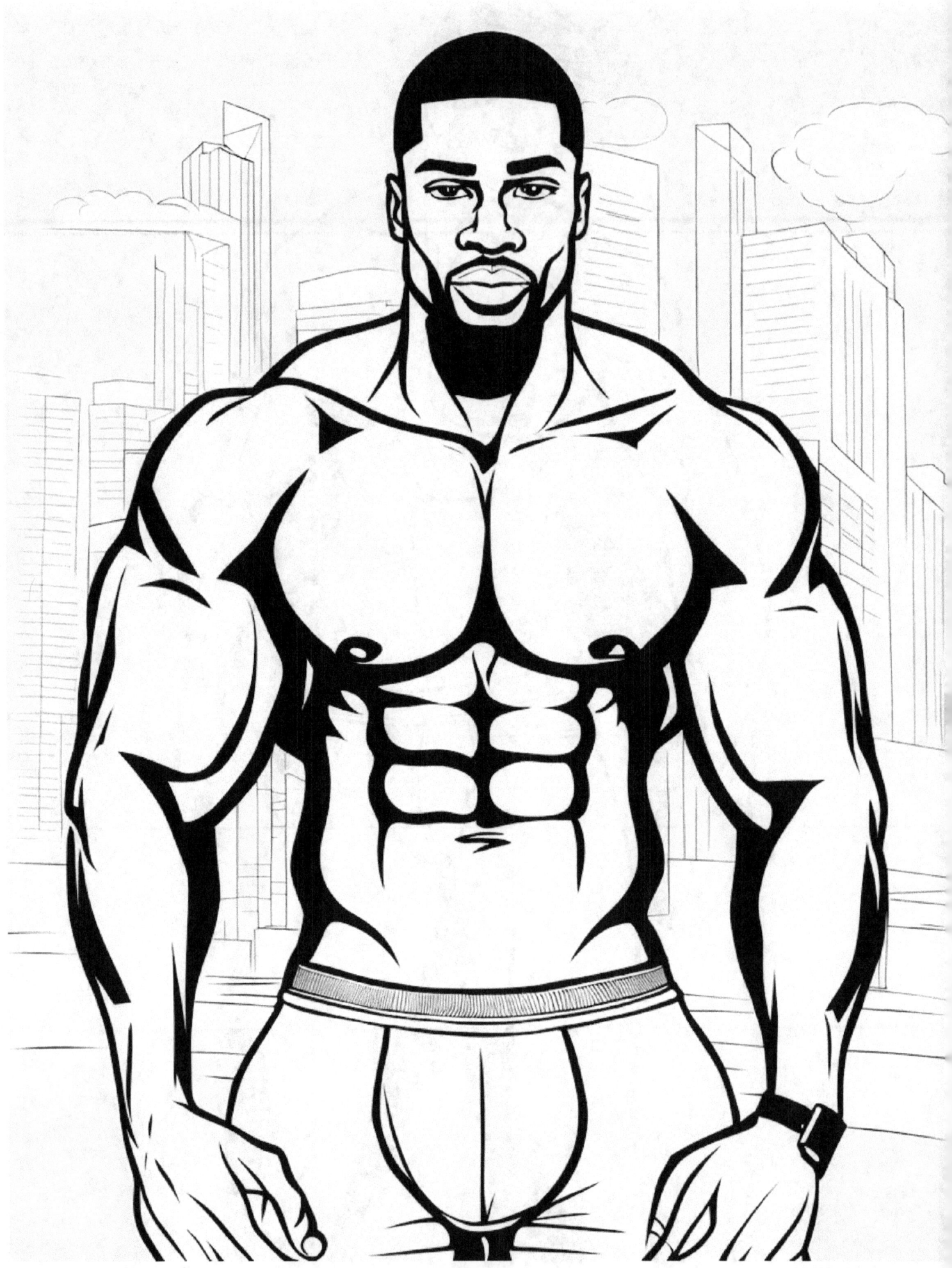

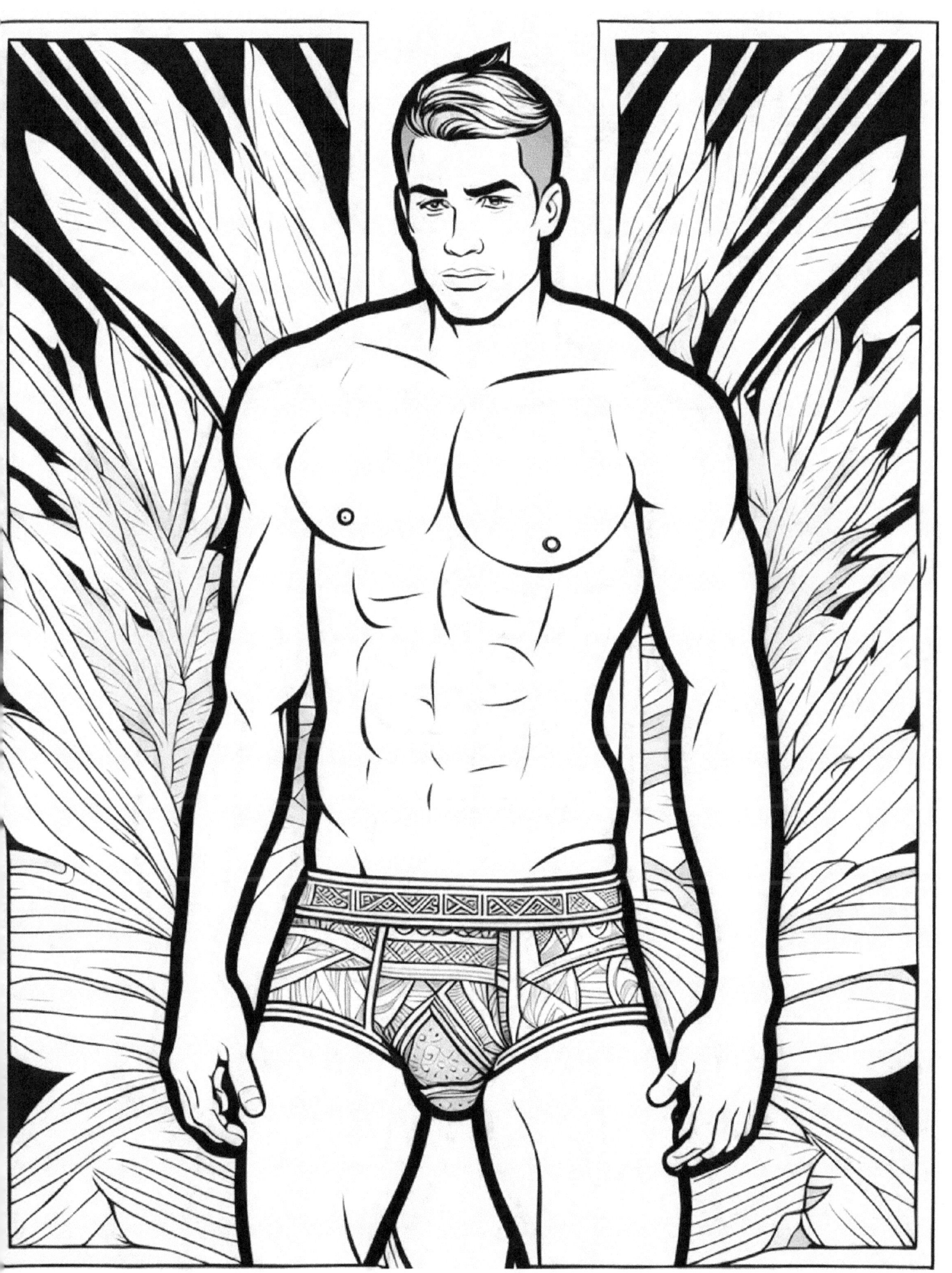

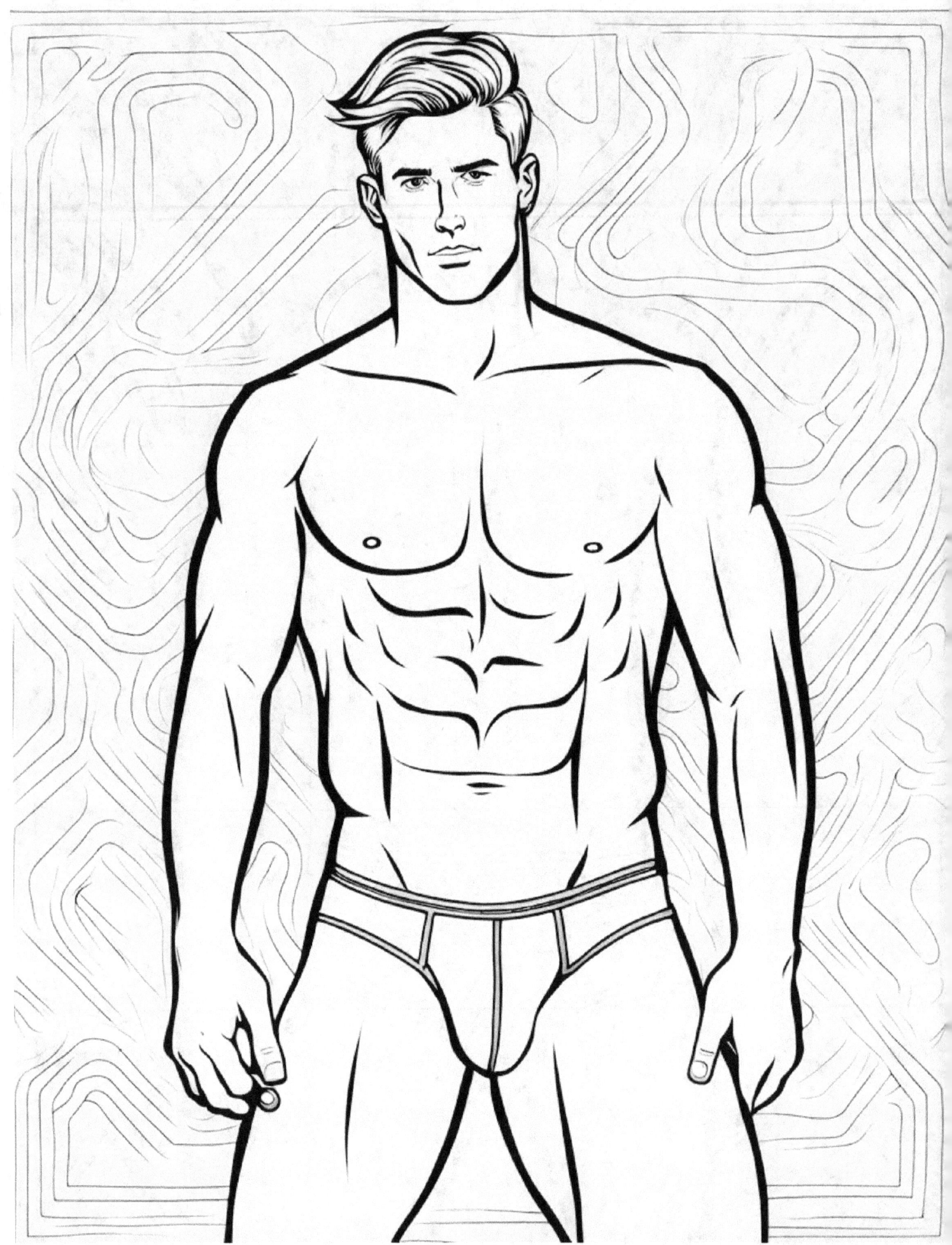

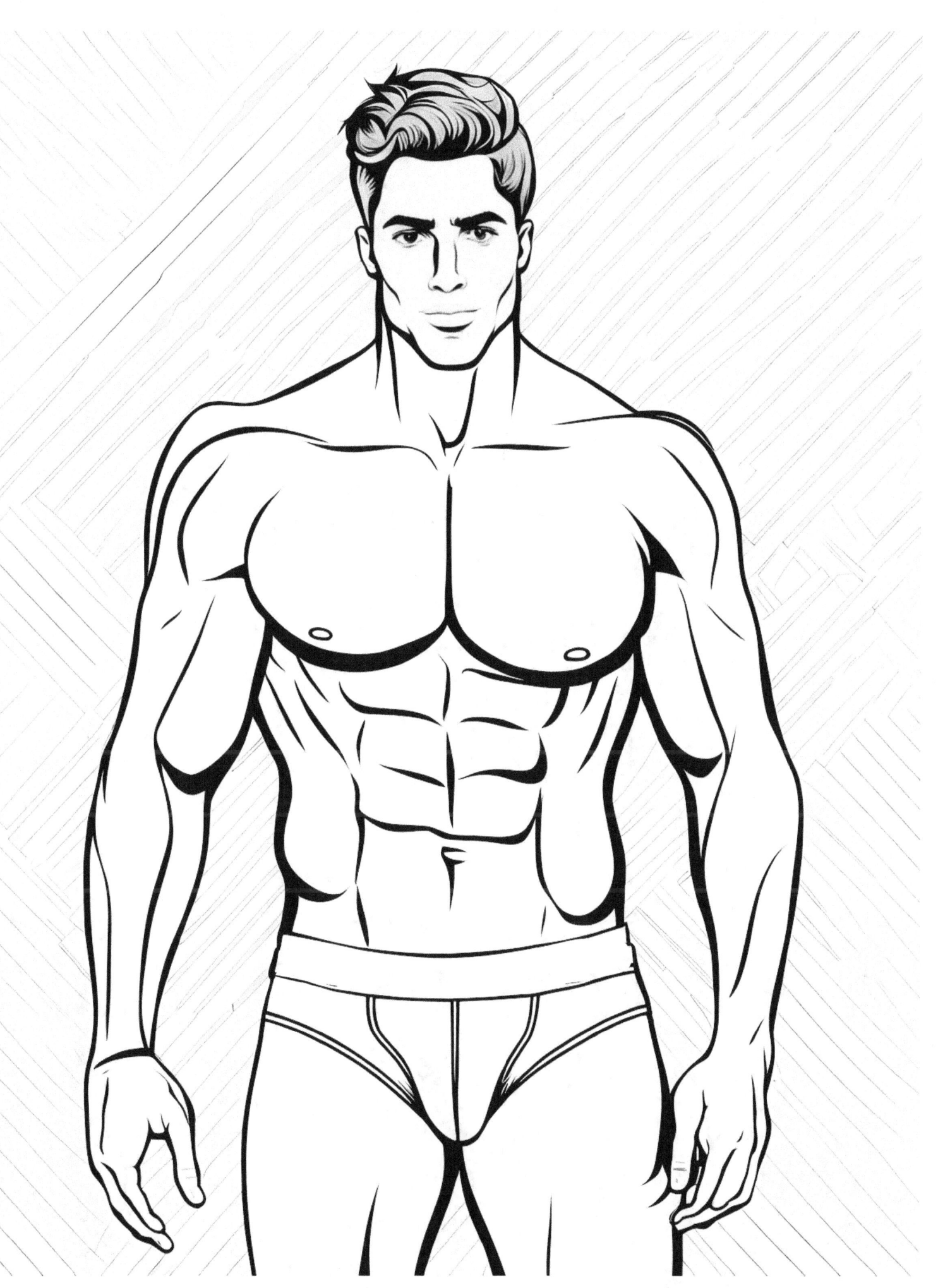

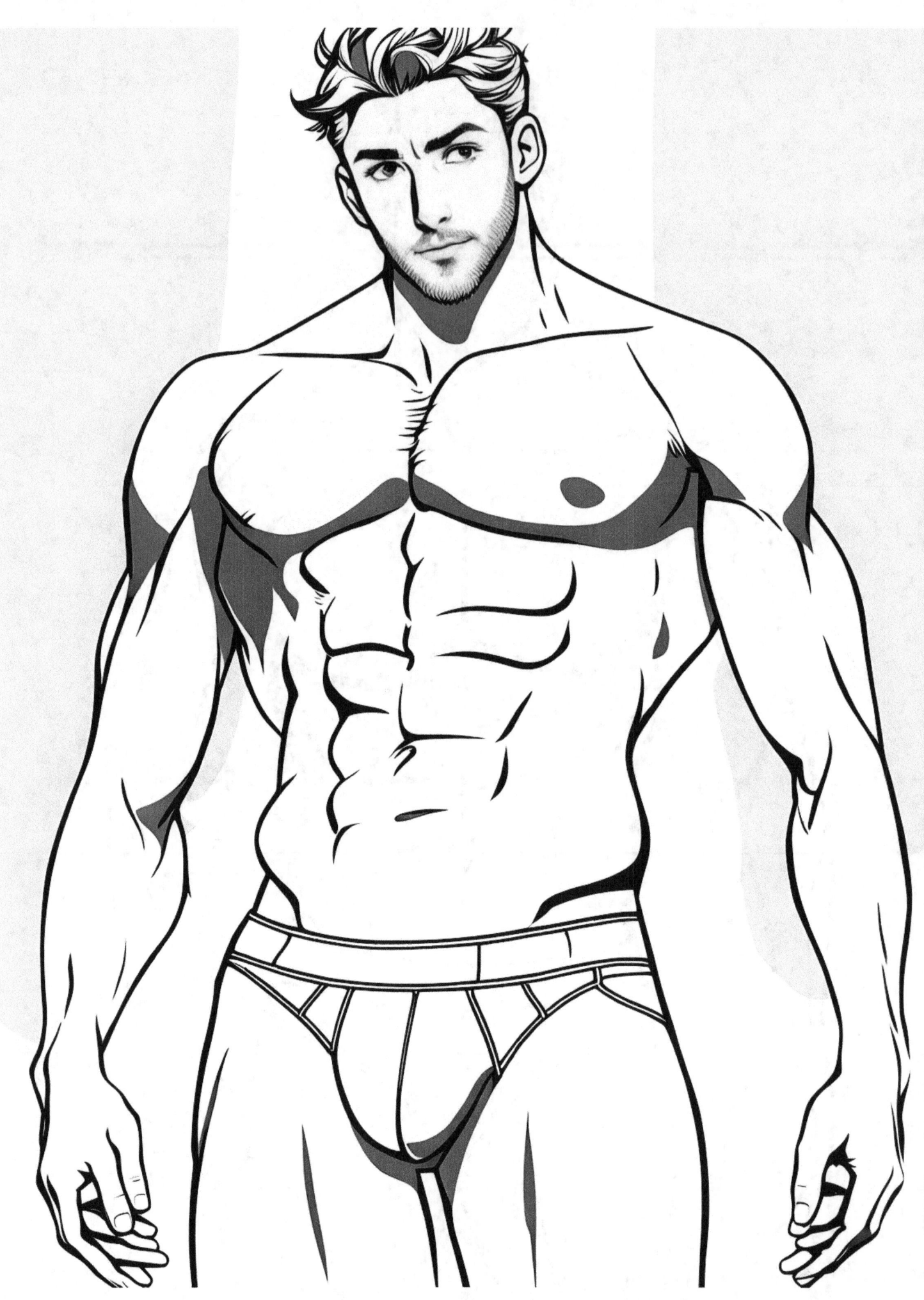

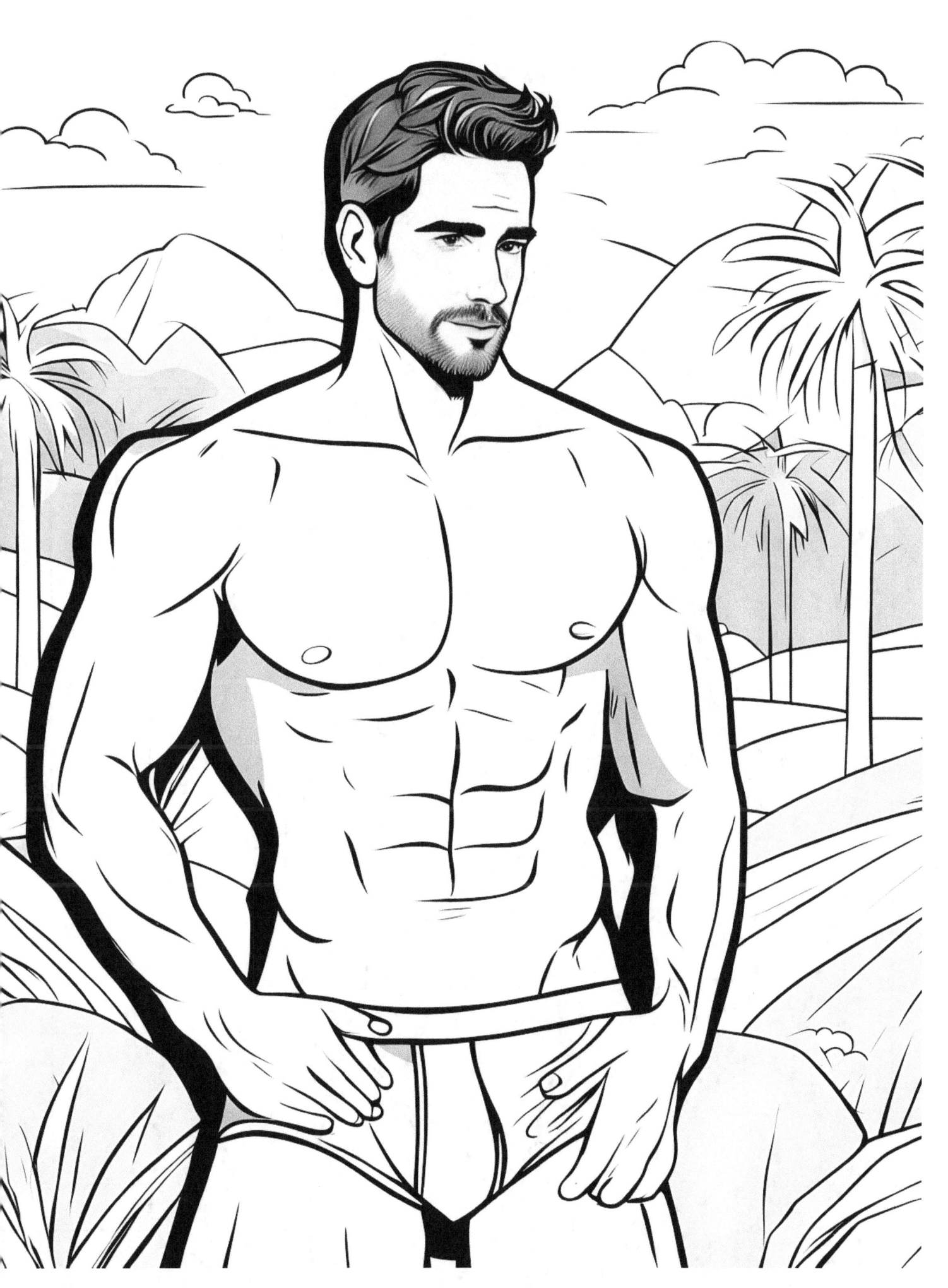

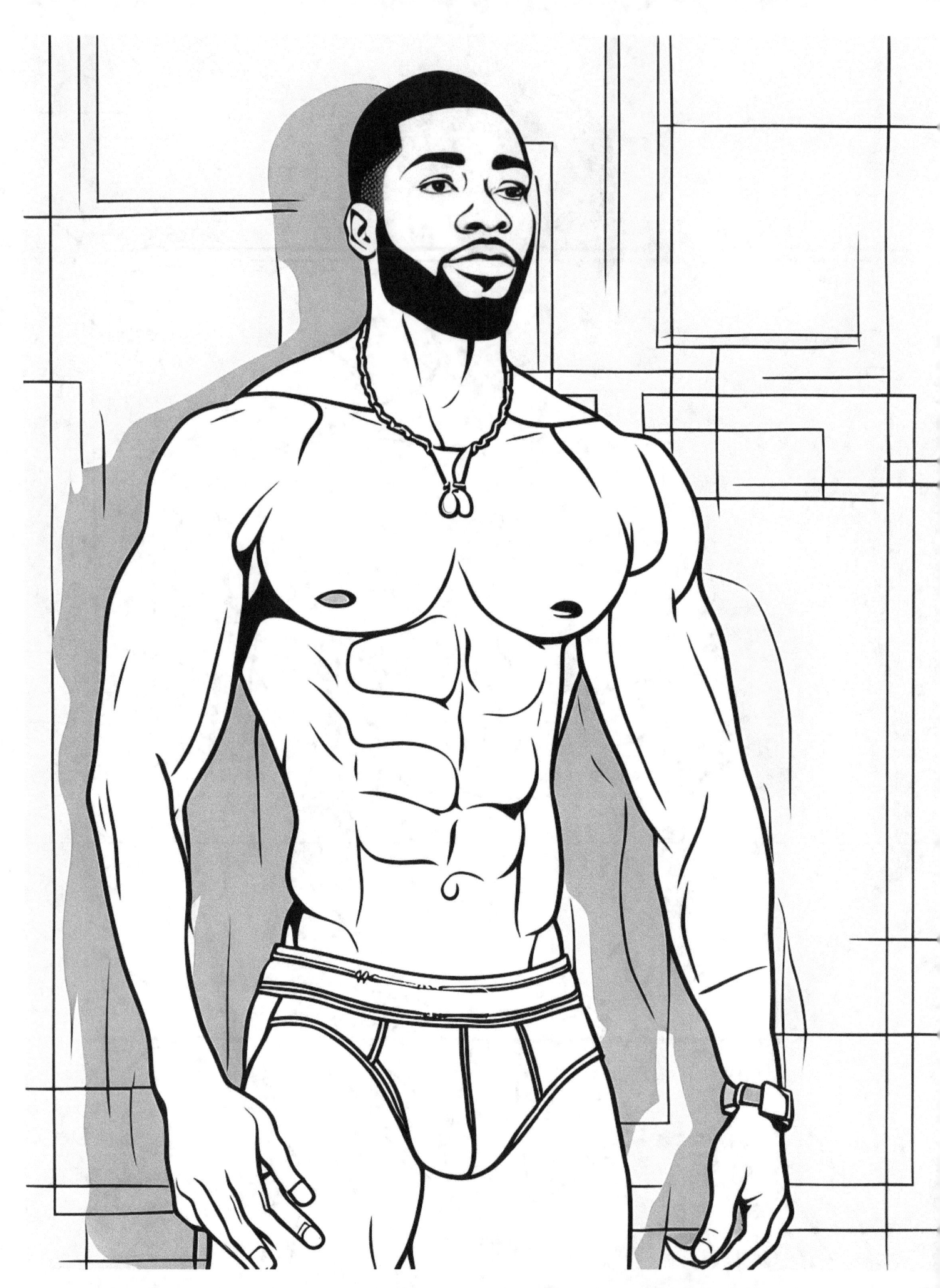

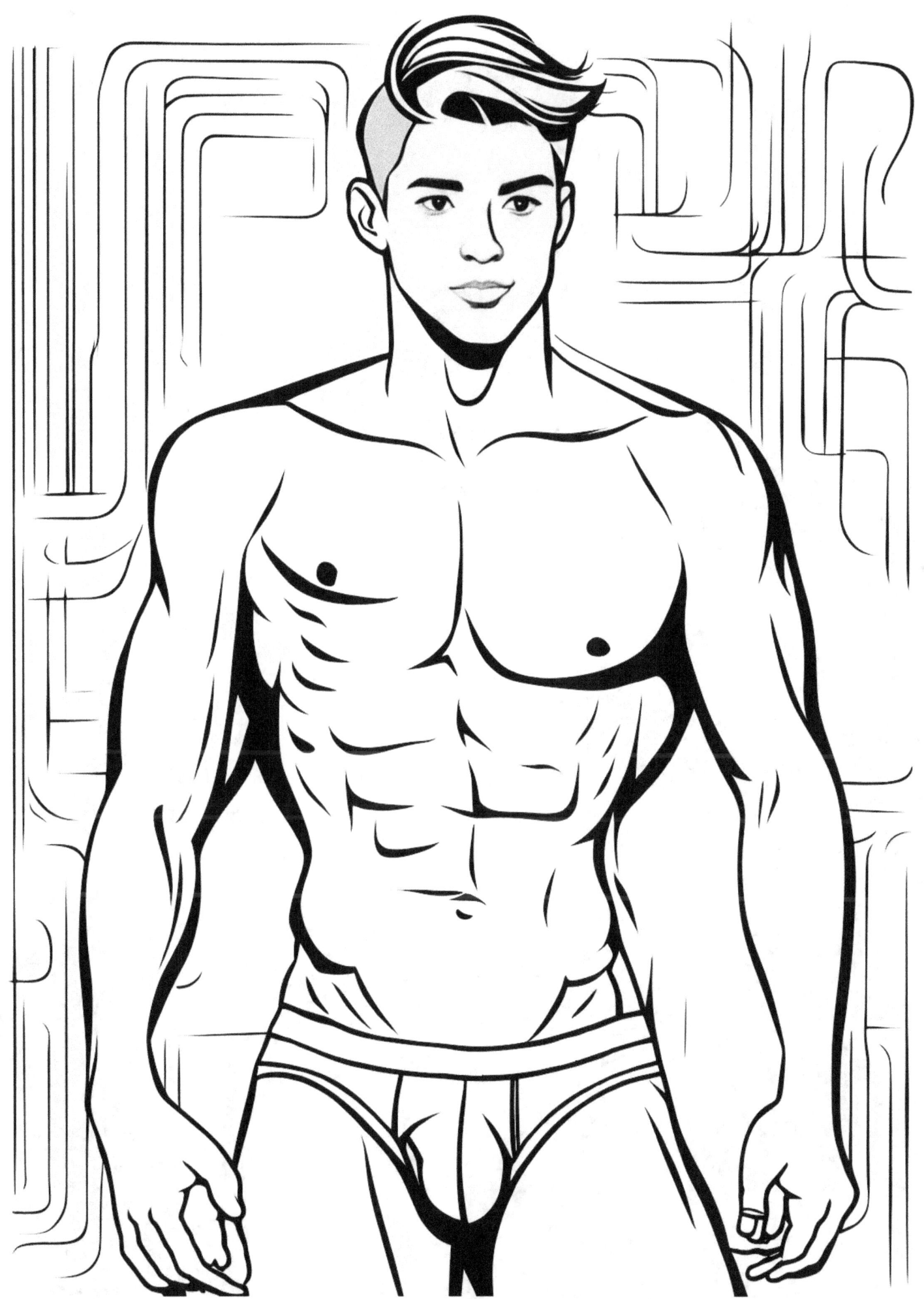

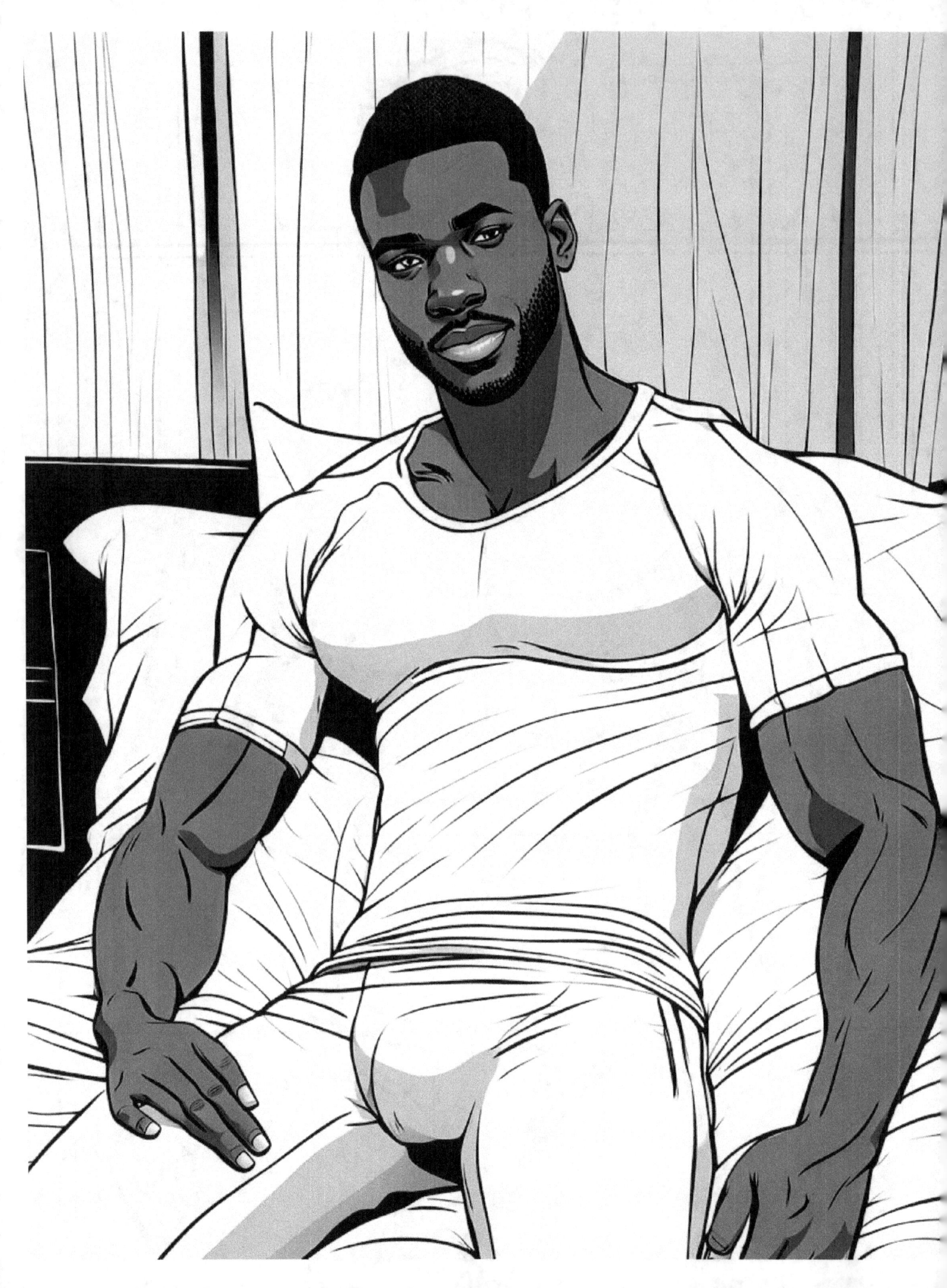

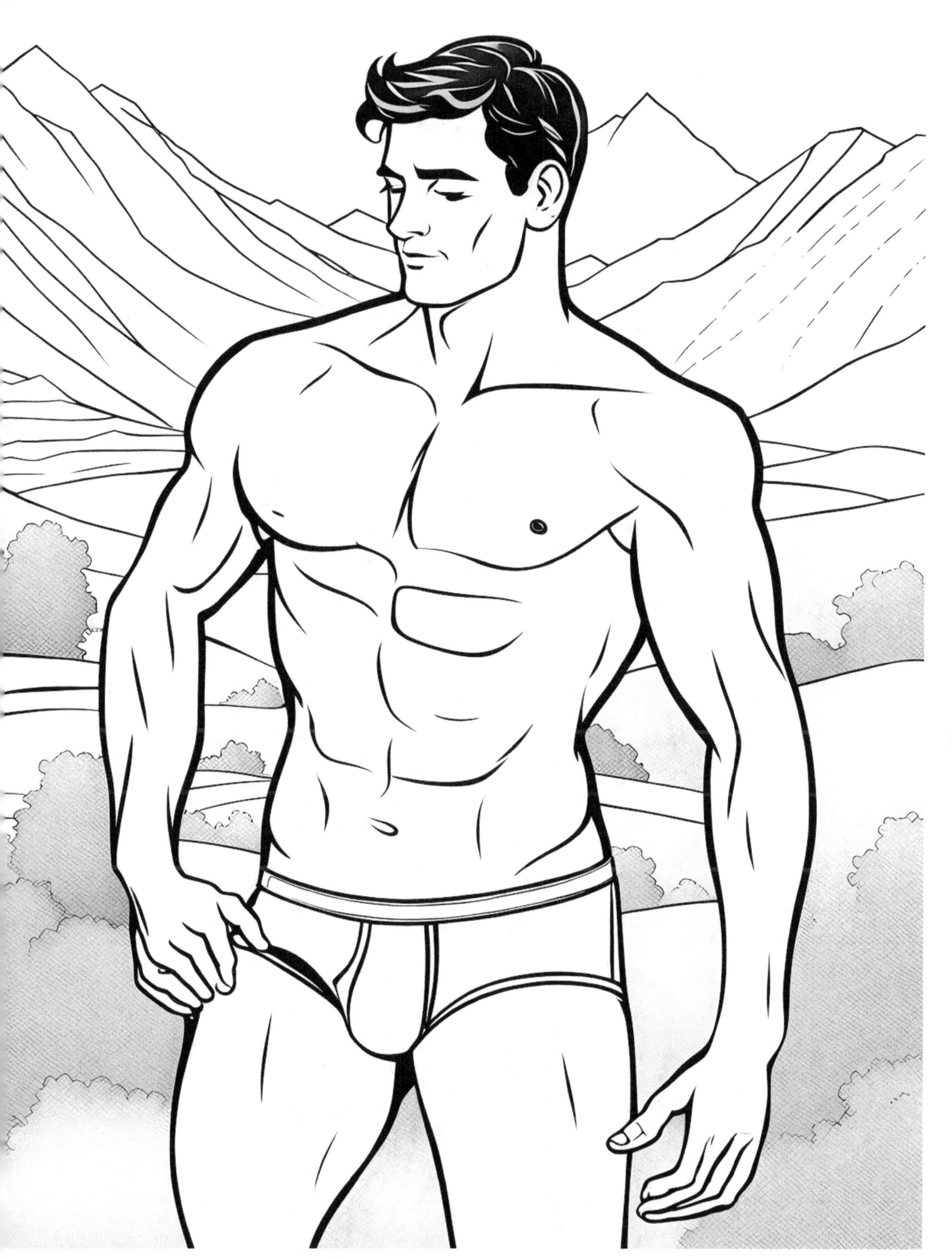

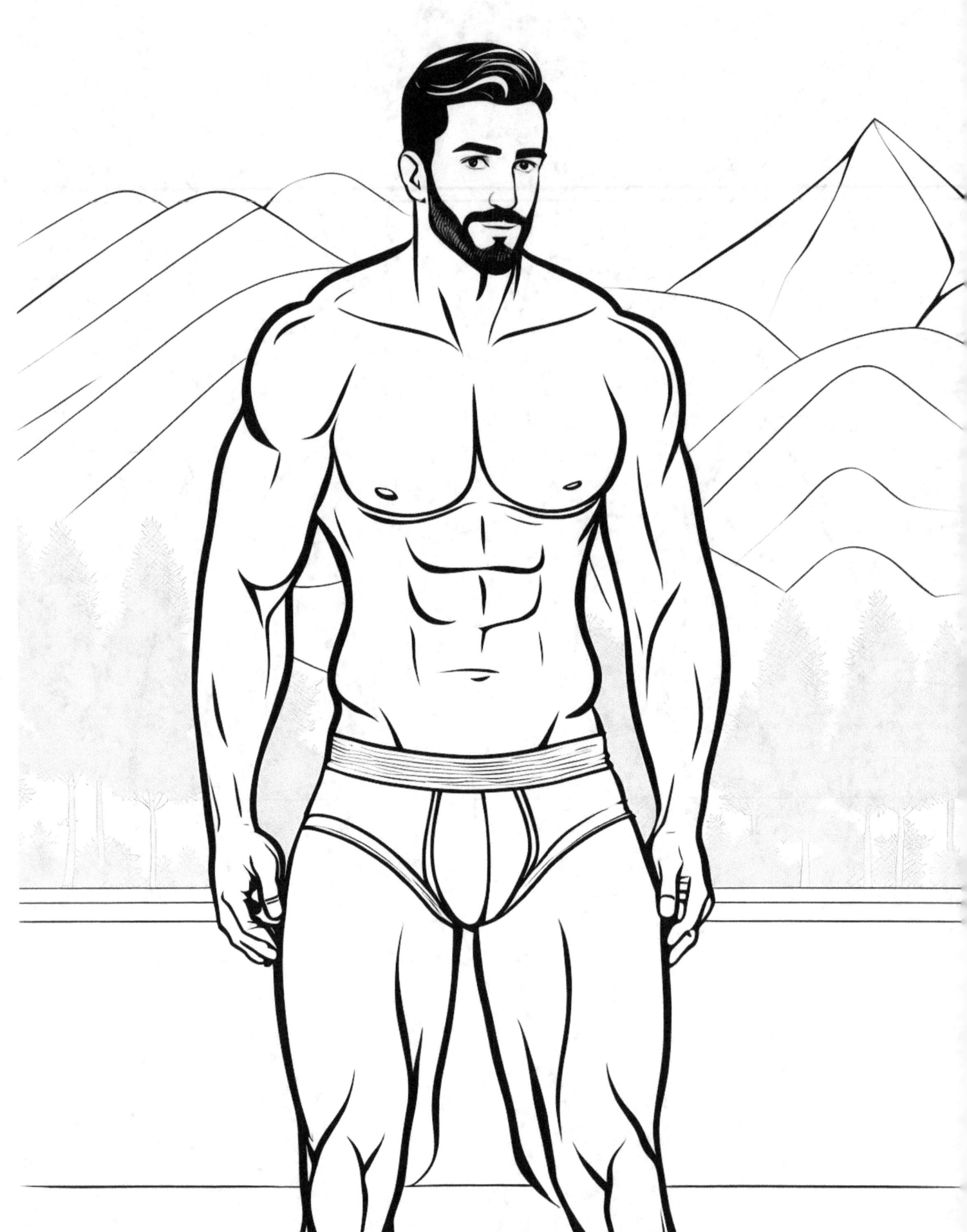

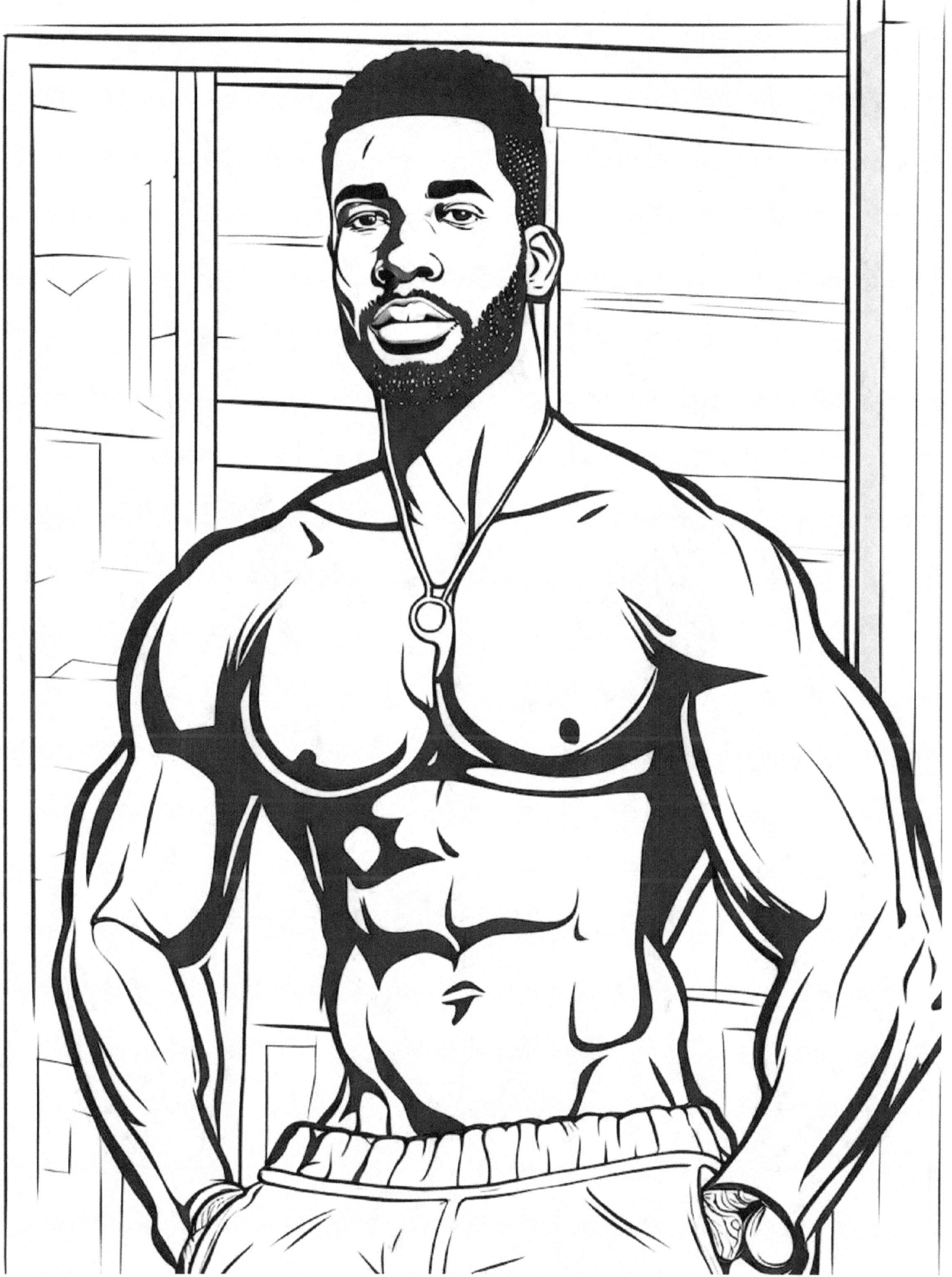

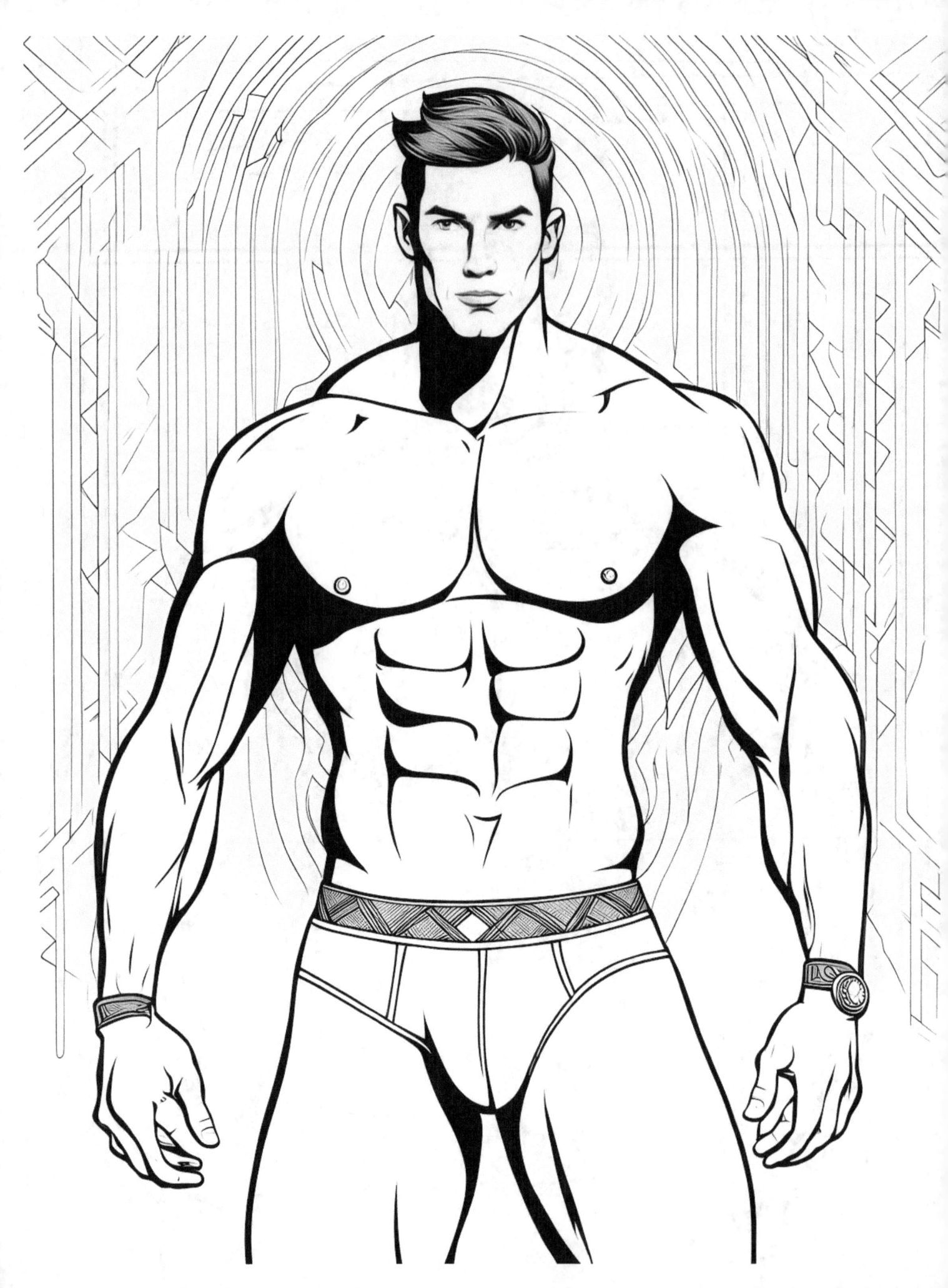

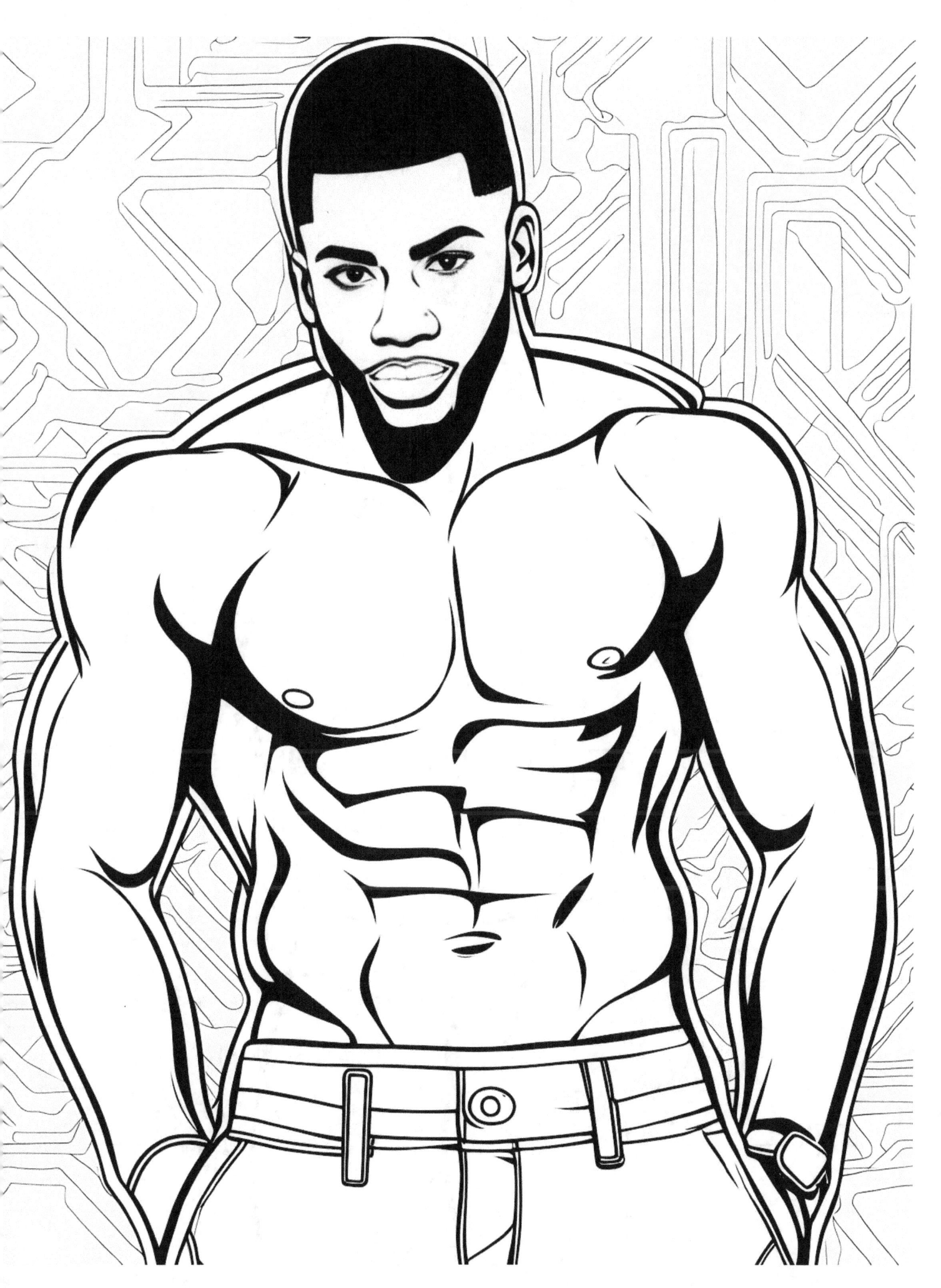

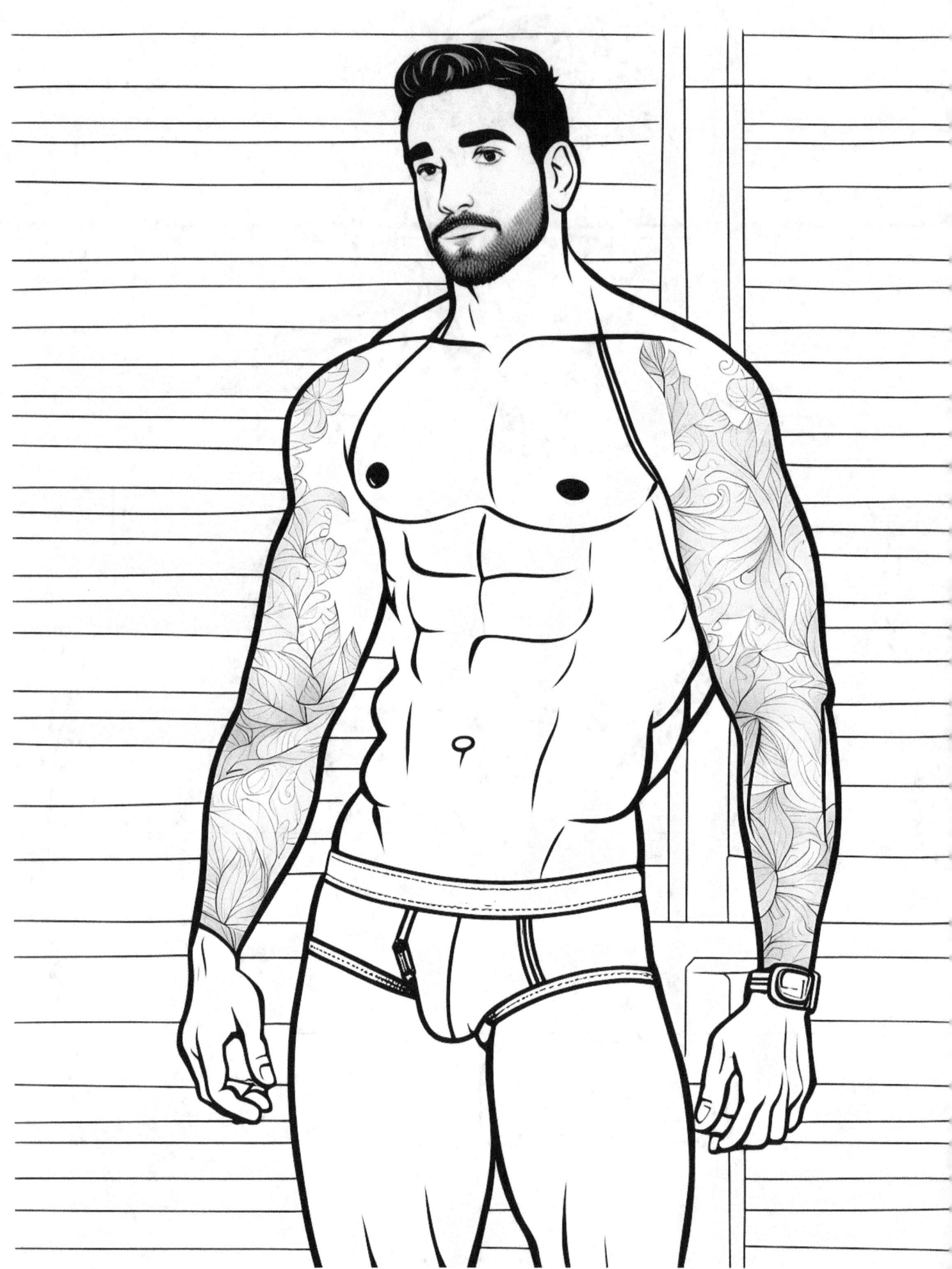

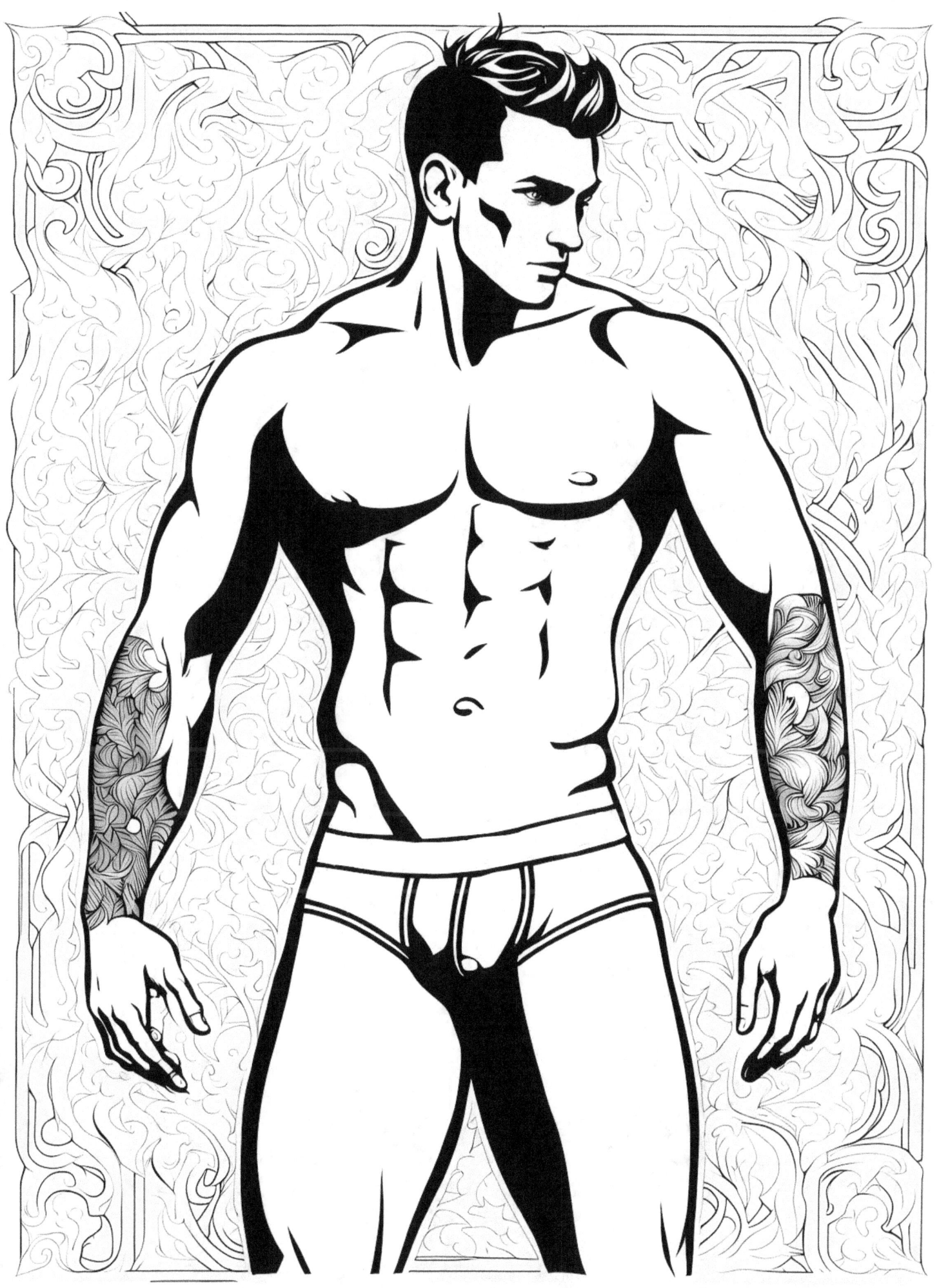

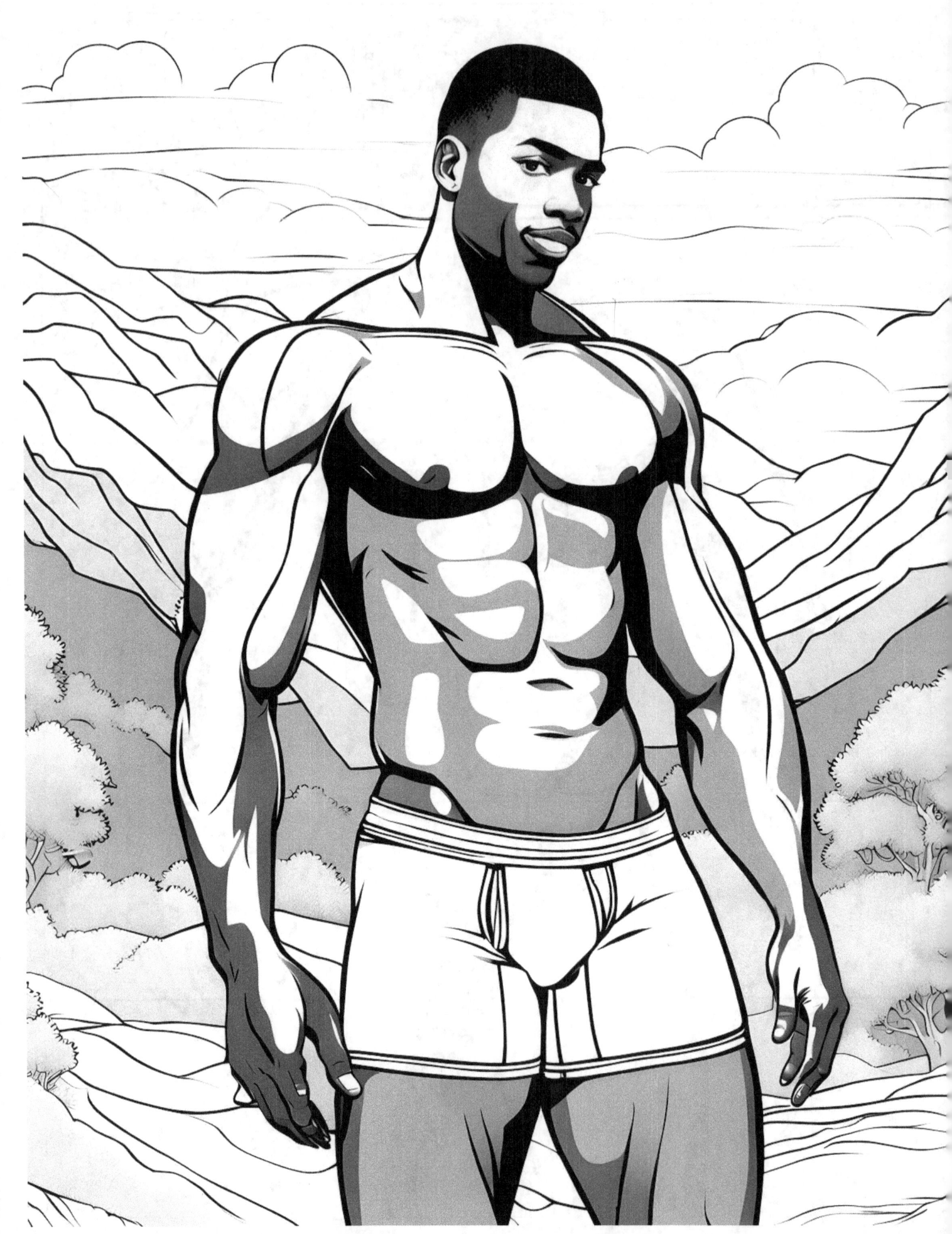

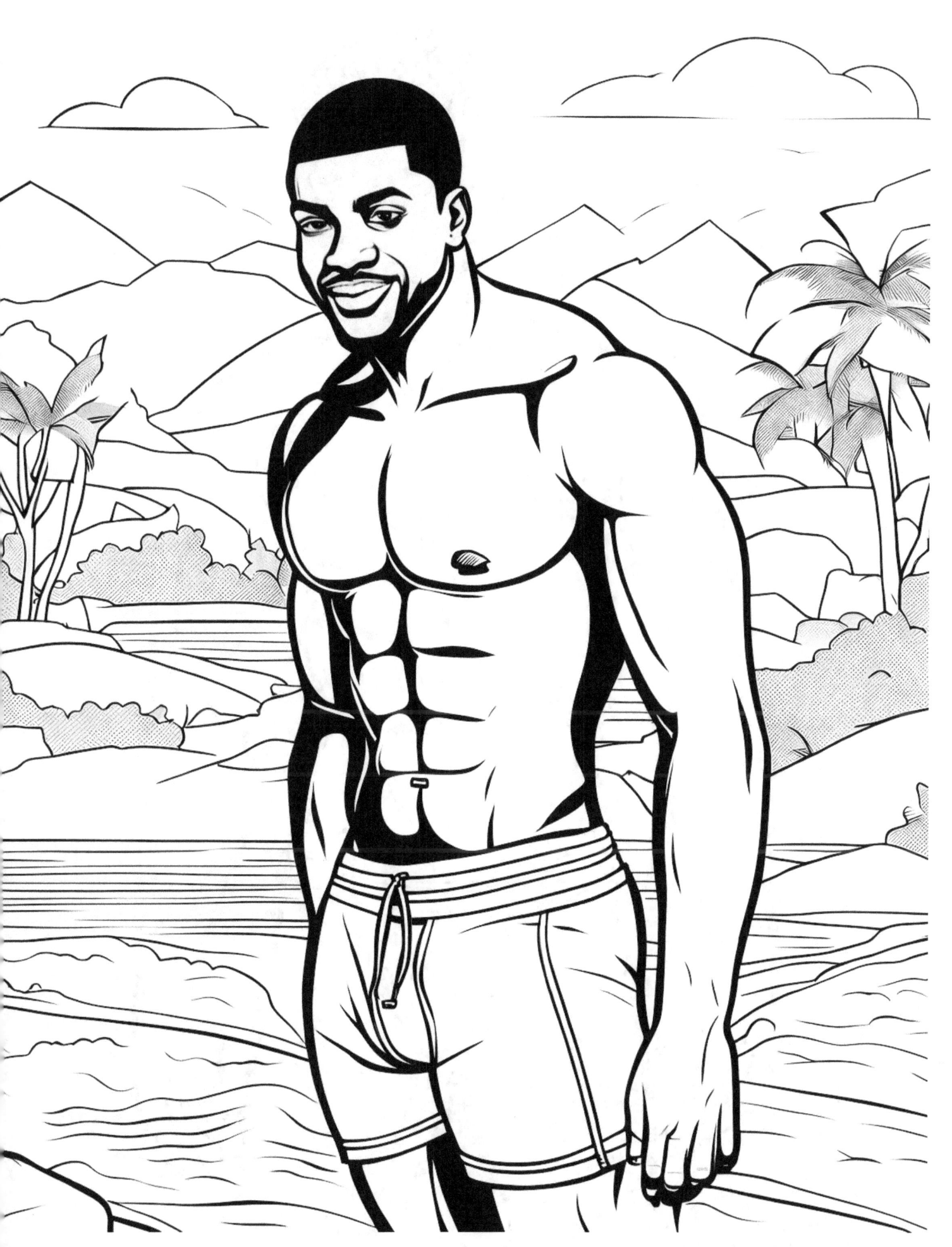

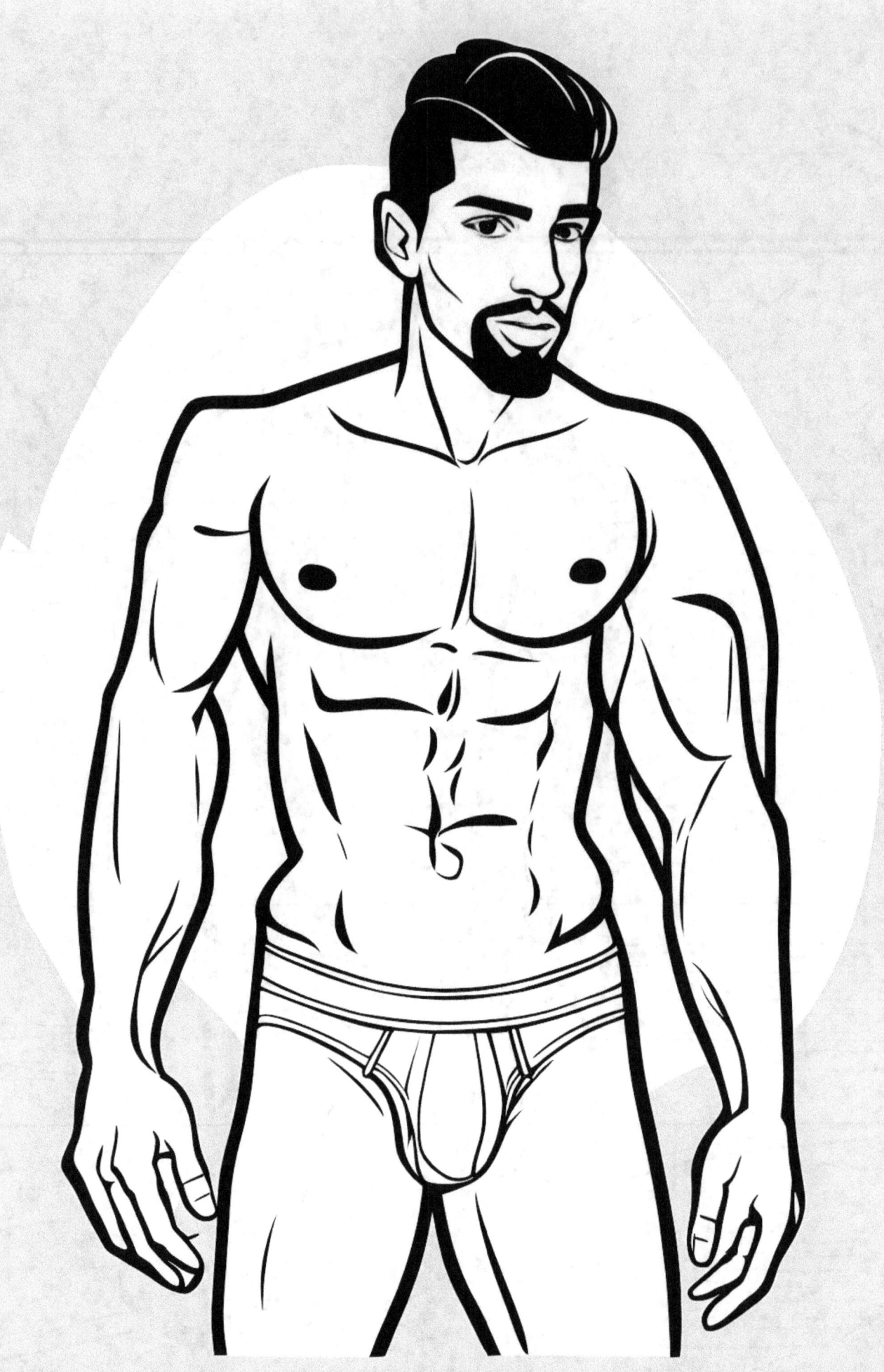

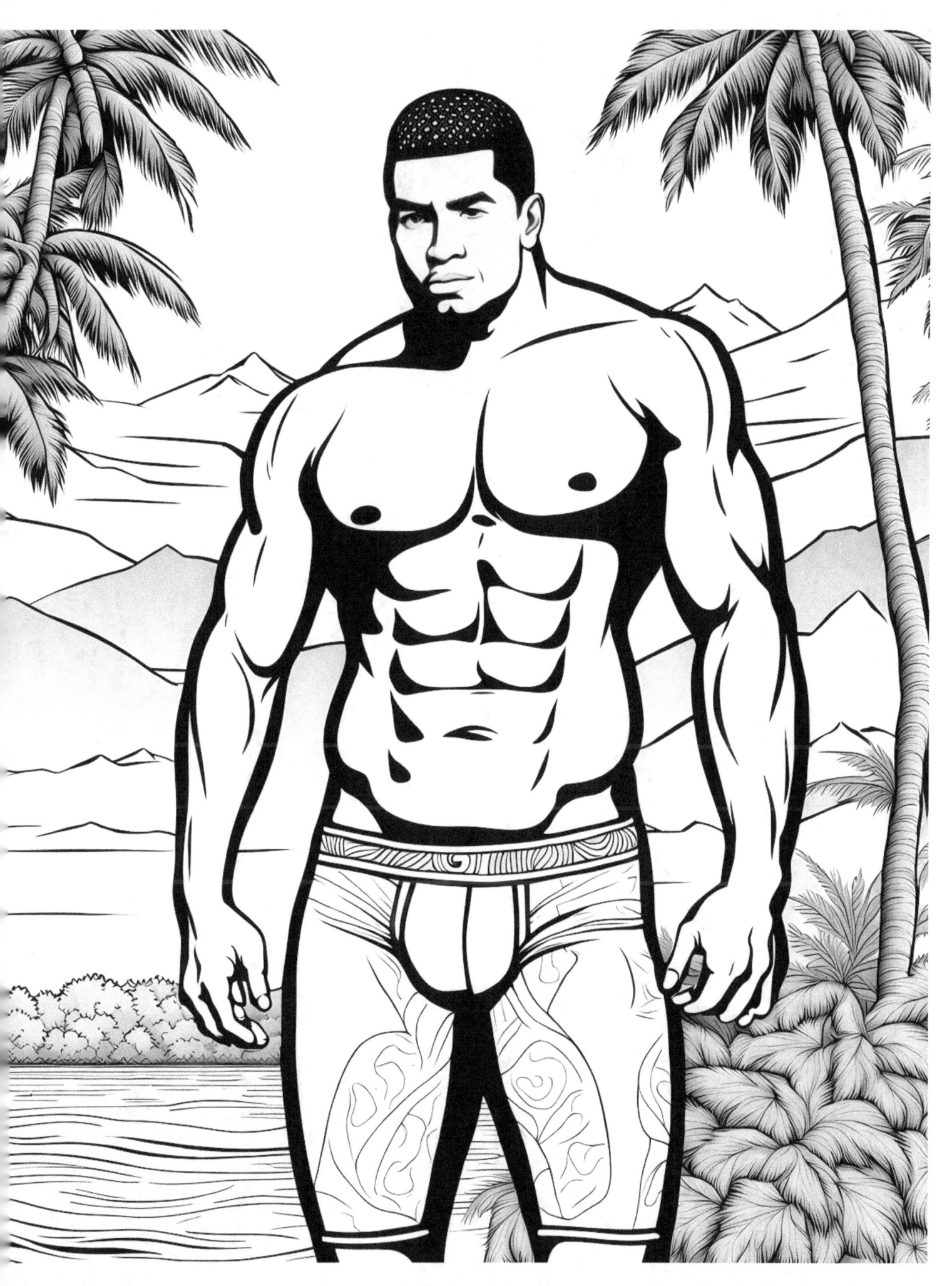

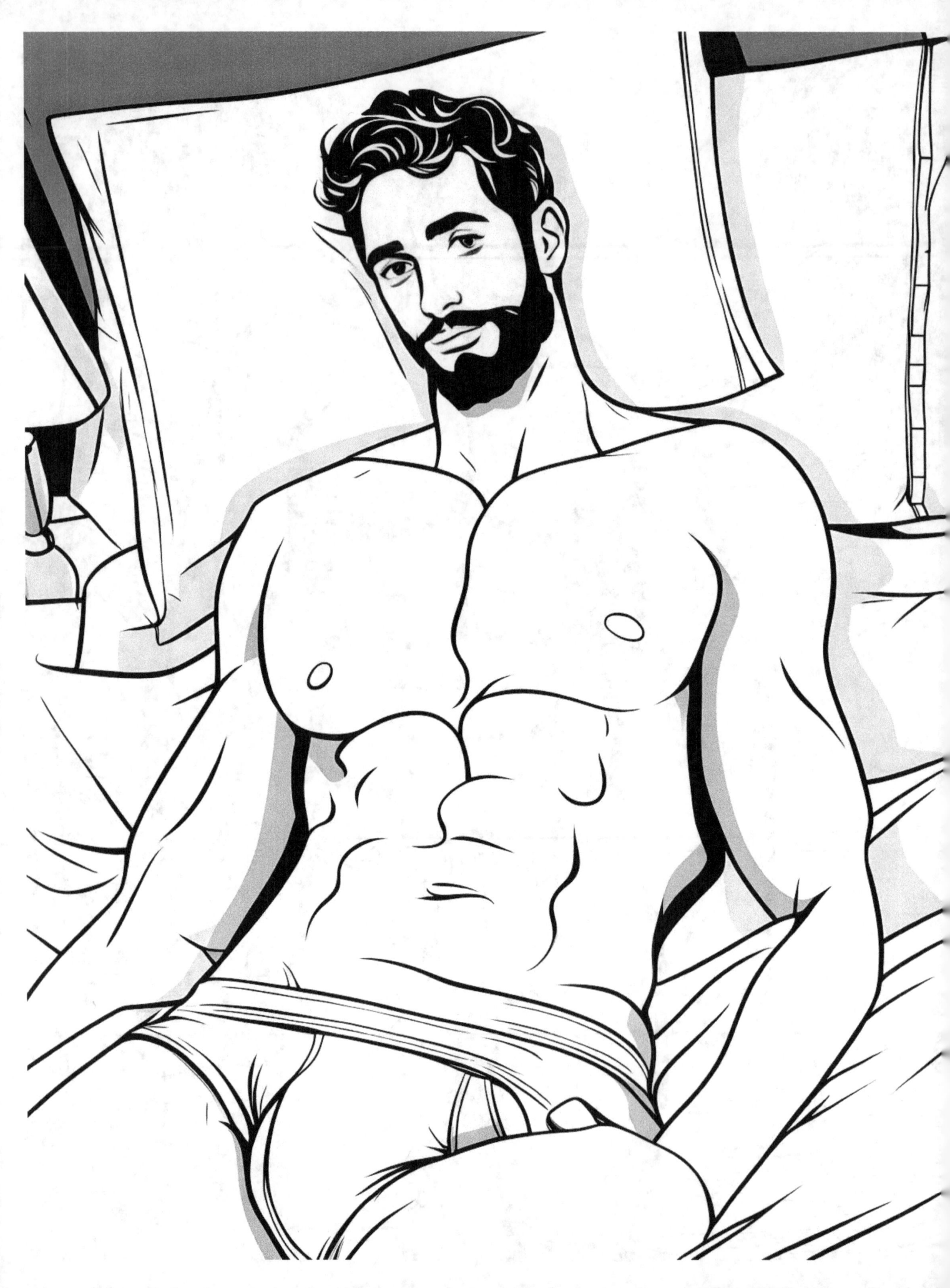

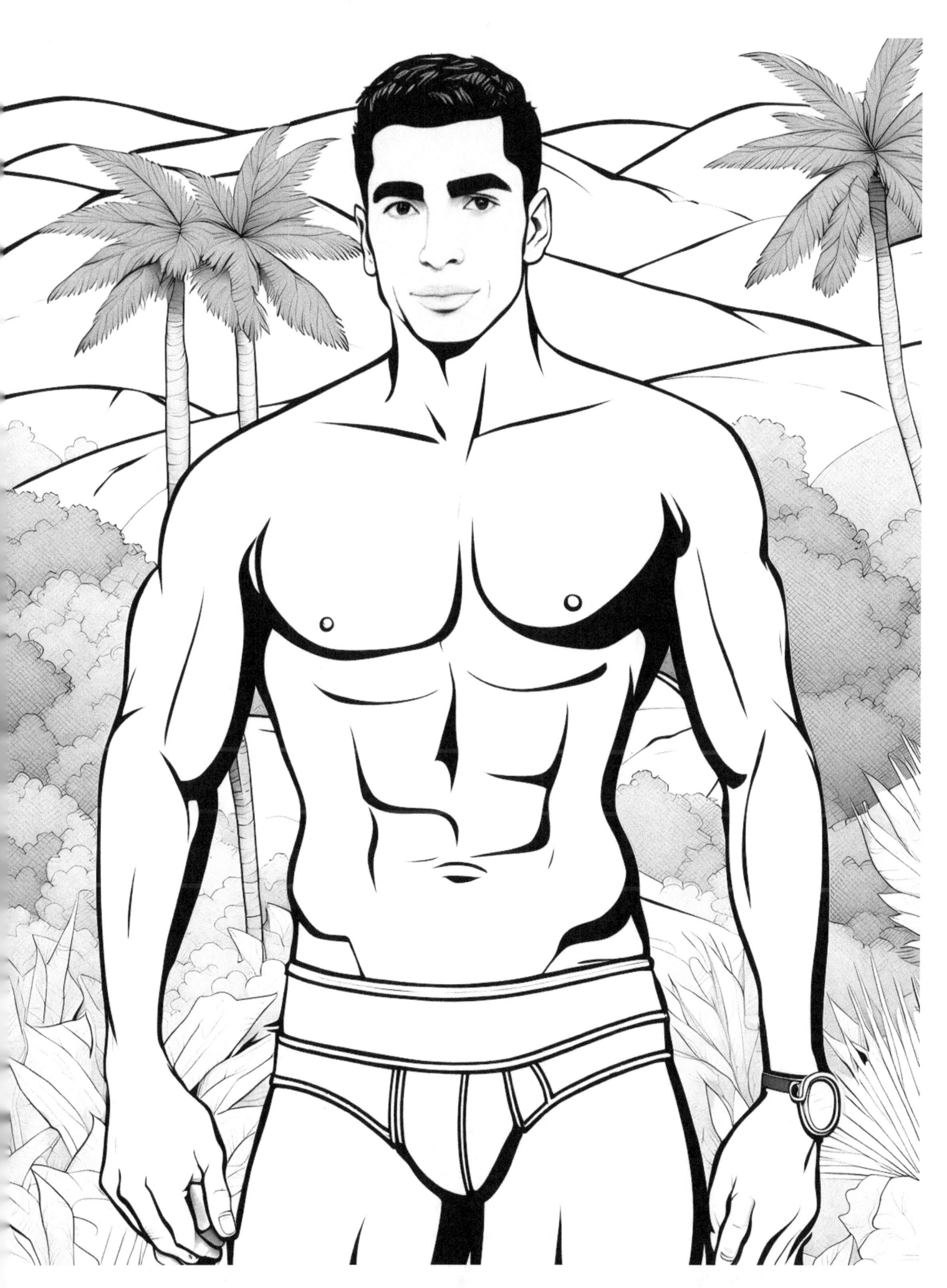

www.ingramcontent.com/pod-product-compliance
Lightning Source LLC
Chambersburg PA
CBHW082220290526

45794CB00009B/3612

*9798859420902*